DAWN OF THE RECONQUEST

Daniel Moorlyn

IRONCLAD
WAR HISTORIES

CONTENTS

Author's Note	V
Crossroads of Conquest	1
The Visigothic Rule	5
Fusion of Worlds	10
Seeds of Dissent	15
Era of Leovigild	20
A Kingdom Divided	24
Society in Strain	28
Fragile Economy	33
An Unsettled Frontier	38
Empire at the Gates	44
The Umayyad Conquest	47
The Fall of Toledo	51
Adapting to New Realities	55
Resistance is Futile	59

Establishment of Al-Andalus   63

Tolerance and Taxation   67

Rise of a Leader   72

Battle of Covadonga   76

Kingdom of Asturias   80

Dynamics of Coexistence   84

Fusion of Knowledge   90

The Political Paradigm   94

New Christian Kingdoms   98

Kingdom of León   101

Castile's Ascendancy   105

Navarre in the Reconquista   110

Crown of Aragon   113

Alliances and Power Dynamics   117

Legacy of the Dawn   123

Timeline of Key Events   126

Bibliography and Sources   130

AUTHOR'S NOTE

I've taken a different approach in presenting this book's historical references and sources. Traditionally, historical texts use footnotes or inline text numbers to cite sources or provide additional context.

While this method is the status quo, I find it an obstacle to the fluidity and enjoyment of reading. I believe that the constant interruption of the main text is a distraction, pulling the reader out of the story. So, I have chosen not to use footnotes and inline citations.

History, especially a subject as rich and intricate as the Reconquista, is not just a collection of facts and dates; it is a story. I aim to present this story in an engaging and uninterrupted manner, allowing readers to journey through the events and lives that shaped this period without interruptions.

Instead of footnotes, I have added a bibliography and a list of sources at the end of this book. This section will not only provide a detailed account of the materials and research utilized in writing this book but will also serve as a guide for further reading and exploration.

By choosing this approach, I hope to offer a seamless and engaging reading experience that honors the narrative flow while still providing the rigorous historical grounding essential to a work of this nature. This book is as much a journey through a pivotal era of history as it is an invitation to further exploration and discovery.

Thank you for joining me on this journey, and I hope you find both enjoyment and enlightenment in these pages.

Daniel Cruzado

Holy War Histories

CROSSROADS OF CONQUEST

In the year 711, as dawn broke over the Strait of Gibraltar, a vanguard of warriors from North Africa under the Umayyad Caliphate set their eyes on the verdant lands of Hispania. The Iberian Peninsula, a collection of cultures and religions under the Visigothic Kingdom, stood on the precipice of a monumental change.

The Visigoths, inheritors of the Roman legacy, had ruled this land with a blend of Roman administrative savvy and Germanic vigor. Yet, internal strife and weakened leadership had frayed the fabric of their kingdom.

The ensuing Islamic conquest, rapid and relentless, overturned the Visigothic dominion in a few short years. It was not merely a military conquest but a transformation of the very soul of Iberia. The Umayyad surge brought new ideas, cultures, and a new religion—Islam—that would intertwine with the existing Christian and Jewish tapestries of the peninsula.

The Reconquista, spanning almost eight centuries, was not just a series of battles and skirmishes to reclaim land. It was a complex dance of power, religion, and culture. Christian kingdoms in the north, initially fragmented and beleaguered, gradually grew in strength and ambition. They saw not just the opportunity to reclaim lost territories but to forge new identities, kingdoms, and, eventually, a unified nation under the banner of Christianity.

This period saw the rise and fall of empires, the clashing and blending of cultures, and the birth of enduring legends. When a simple cave in Covadonga became the cradle of resistance, a nobleman named Pelayo rallied a band of fighters to strike the first blow for Christian reconquest. It was a time when the magnificent city of Córdoba became a beacon of learning and culture, illuminating the Dark Ages of Europe.

But the Reconquista was more than a mere clash of civilizations. It was a breeding ground for art, architecture, science, and literature. The intermingling of Muslim, Christian, and Jewish traditions created a unique cultural landscape, from the haunting verses of Andalusian poetry to the awe-inspiring arches of the Great Mosque of Córdoba.

As the sun set on the Visigothic rule, the stage was set for an era of transformation. The Umayyad conquest did not merely redraw the borders of the Iberian Peninsula; it rewrote its destiny. The Islamic tide brought with it not only warriors but scholars, artisans, and a new worldview that would intertwine with the existing fabric of Iberian society.

The initial shock of the conquest gave way to a period of relative stability under the Umayyads. The city of Córdoba, under the enlightened rule of Abd al-Rahman III, emerged as a jewel of the medieval world, rivaling the grandeur of Constantinople and Baghdad. Here, in the bustling streets and vibrant markets, Muslims, Christians, and Jews coexisted, contributing to a flourishing of culture and knowledge. The famed Library of Córdoba housed countless scrolls, a testament to the Islamic world's reverence for learning.

Yet, beneath this veneer of unity and progress, the seeds of resistance were sprouting in the northern fringes of the peninsula. In the rugged mountains of Asturias, a Visigothic nobleman named Pelayo refused to yield to the new order. The Battle of Covadonga, though a minor skirmish in military terms, was a beacon of hope for Christian resistance. It was here that the legend of the Reconquista truly began, a legend that would inspire generations to come.

The Christian kingdoms, initially fragmented, began to consolidate power. The Kingdom of Asturias slowly expanded, giving rise to the Kingdom of León. To the east, the Kingdom of Navarre carved out its realm. The counties of the Spanish March, under the influence of the Frankish Empire, laid the foundation for what would become the Kingdom of Aragon and the County of Barcelona.

As these Christian realms grew in strength, so did their ambition. The Reconquista became more than a defensive struggle; it evolved into a crusade to reclaim lost lands. The frontier between

Muslim and Christian territories, known as the "Marches," was a dynamic and often chaotic region where allegiances shifted, and battles were fought not just for territory but for honor and redemption.

The Reconquista was punctuated by iconic moments: the capture of Toledo in 1085, a city of immense symbolic and strategic value; the fall of Lisbon in 1147, a testament to the growing power of the Portuguese; and the victory at Las Navas de Tolosa in 1212, a turning point that marked the decline of Muslim power in the peninsula.

Yet, the true essence of the Reconquista lies in its enduring impact on the people of Iberia. This period saw the emergence of the Spanish and Portuguese identities, the forging of national myths, and the shaping of religious and cultural landscapes that continue to define the region. Though often fraught with tension, the convivencia, or coexistence of different faiths and cultures, left a legacy of artistic and intellectual richness.

The Reconquista, with its blend of heroism, tragedy, and perseverance, is not just a chapter in the history of Spain and Portugal. It is a saga that resonates with universal themes of conflict, coexistence, ambition, and resistance, shaping identity and legacy.

During this tumultuous period, we gain insights into the enduring question of how societies and cultures evolve, clash, and, ultimately, transform.

THE VISIGOTHIC RULE

As the Roman Empire's grasp on Hispania waned, the Visigoths, a people of Germanic origin, emerged as the new stewards of this land. Initially serving as *foederati* or allied mercenaries of Rome, they carved out a domain for themselves, setting the stage for a unique era in Iberian history. Their ascendancy in the early 5th century marked a change in rulership and a blending of two worlds - the ancient Roman and the burgeoning Germanic.

The Visigothic political structure was an intriguing blend of Roman imperial traditions and Germanic tribal customs. Visigothic kings, much like Roman emperors, wielded considerable authority. They were the central figures in the kingdom, arbiters of law, and military leaders. Yet, the realities of ruling a diverse and geographically fragmented realm often checked their power.

While embracing the ceremonials and pomp reminiscent of Roman emperors, these kings also adhered to Germanic practices. Leadership was often a matter of personal charisma and military prowess, reflecting the Germanic tradition of warrior kingship. This duality in governance created a unique political landscape where Roman administrative acumen met the spirited independence of the Germanic tribal system.

Despite the changes in leadership, the administrative skeleton of the Roman Empire continued to influence Hispania. The Visigoths adopted many Roman administrative practices, recognizing the efficiency of the Roman bureaucratic system. Cities remained centers of administration, and the Roman legal framework continued to shape laws and governance.

Latin, the language of the Romans, remained the lingua franca of administration and liturgy. This persistence of Latin facilitated the continuity of Roman culture and laid the groundwork for the development of the Romance languages, including what would become Spanish and Portuguese.

One of the most significant legacies of this era was the legal code developed under the Visigoths. Drawing on Roman law, the Visigothic Code attempted to unify the diverse populace under a common legal framework. This code was revolutionary in its attempt to apply laws uniformly to the Gothic and Roman populations, a bold undertaking in a world rife with ethnic divisions.

In religion, the Visigothic Kingdom initially followed Arian Christianity, distinct from the Roman Catholicism of the majority Hispano-Roman population. However, the eventual conversion of the Visigoths to Catholicism under King Reccared in the late 6th century was a turning point, aligning the kingdom more closely with the religious practices of its Roman subjects.

The Visigothic Kingdom in Hispania was a realm where the echoes of Rome resonated amidst the flourishing Germanic spirit. This period, often overlooked, was crucial in shaping the Iberian Peninsula's historical trajectory. It was when the remnants of a great empire met the vitality of a rising culture.

The legacy of this era, marked by a fusion of Roman and Germanic influences, set the stage for the tumultuous centuries to come, eventually leading to the dramatic events of the Reconquista.

***

The Visigothic Hispania societal structure was undergoing a profound transformation. The nobility, a class composed of both Visigothic and Hispano-Roman elites, stood at the forefront of this change. Visigothic nobles, often warriors or leaders who had gained prominence through feats of arms or loyalty to the king, brought with them the Germanic traditions of leadership and honor. In contrast, the Hispano-Roman aristocracy carried the legacy of Roman administrative skills and land management.

This culture clash within the nobility created a unique dynamic. While sharing power, the Visigothic and Roman elites often had differing visions for the kingdom, leading to political intrigues and power struggles. These tensions sometimes manifested in open challenges to the kings' authority as various factions vied for influence. While a central figure, the king had to navigate this complex web of noble interests to maintain control and ensure stability.

The Church emerged as a significant force in this period, mediating between the Germanic rulers and the Romanized populace. Many of the bishops from the Hispano-Roman elite played a crucial role in the kingdom's political and social life. They were spiritual leaders and advisors to kings, diplomats, and, at times, arbitrators in disputes.

The Church's influence was partly due to its role as the guardian of Roman Christian traditions, which appealed to the Hispano-Roman population. With the Visigothic conversion to Catholicism, the Church also gained the patronage of the kings, further solidifying its position. This growing ecclesiastical power was evident in the Councils of Toledo, where bishops, nobles, and the king convened to discuss matters of state and Church.

****

The lives of the common people in Visigothic Hispania reflected the evolving cultures. The majority were Hispano-Romans, descendants of the Roman inhabitants, and their lives were still guided mainly by Roman traditions and practices. Agriculture continued to be the mainstay of the economy, with the rural populace farming the lands that were now under new masters.

The agricultural landscape was a mix of large estates, some of which continued to operate under the Roman *latifundia* system, and smaller farms influenced by Germanic practices. The Visigoths, having a background in a more tribal and less urbanized society, introduced new approaches to land ownership and farming, which gradually permeated the rural landscape.

The common people, whether working on vast estates or smaller farms, faced the uncertainties of a society in transition. The decisions of nobles and kings, the edicts of the Church, and the ever-present undercurrents of cultural integration and friction influenced their lives. Yet, through their labor and daily lives, they continued the legacy of Roman agricultural practices while adapting to the new order brought by the Visigoths.

Visigothic Hispania was a society marked by the interplay of different cultures, social classes, and political ambitions. The nobility, balancing their power between loyalty to the king and their interests; the Church, straddling the line between spiritual authority and temporal influence; and the common people, living their lives under the shadow of these greater forces, together wove the complex tapestry of a kingdom at the crossroads of history. This medley of cultures and traditions set the stage for the dramatic events that would unfold in the centuries to come, leading to the era-defining Reconquista.

FUSION OF WORLDS

The cultural landscape of Visigothic Hispania was where Rome's artistic and architectural legacies met the emerging Germanic sensibilities—this period witnessed a remarkable synthesis in art and architecture, which became emblematic of the Visigothic era.

In art, the fusion is most notably seen in the craftsmanship of items like the votive crowns and the treasure of Guarrazar. These treasures, discovered in a hoard near Toledo, exemplify the blending of artistic traditions. The crowns and crosses, made of gold and encrusted with precious stones and pearls, display a sophistication and intricacy that speak of Roman influences. Yet, their designs also incorporate Germanic elements, such as the *cloisonné* technique and the symbolism imbued in the jewels and inscriptions. These artifacts are not just items of wealth and beauty; they are visual narratives of a society in transition, showcasing the melding of two artistic worlds.

Architecture during the Visigothic period also reflects this cultural synthesis. Though few have survived, buildings from this era indicate a blend of Roman structural techniques with Germanic and early Christian motifs. Horseshoe arches, which would later influence Islamic architecture in Iberia, can be traced back to this period. For instance, the Basilica of San Juan de Baños stands as a testament to this architectural fusion, combining a Roman basilica layout with Visigothic decorative elements.

The religious landscape in Visigothic Hispania was marked by significant evolution and change. Christianity, well-established by the time of the Visigoths' arrival, underwent a period of transformation under their rule. The Visigoths, initially adherents of Arian Christianity, which differed from the Trinitarian doctrine of the Roman Catholic Church, ruled over a predominantly Catholic population.

This religious difference was a matter of theological debate and a source of social and political tension. The Arianism belief system, with its emphasis on the distinctness of the Father and Son in the Trinity, put the Visigothic rulers at odds with the Catholic majority and the influential Catholic Church hierarchy.

The eventual conversion of the Visigothic ruling class to Catholicism under King Reccared in the late 6th century was a pivotal moment in the kingdom's history. This conversion was a strategic move to unify the kingdom under a single religious banner and to reconcile the Germanic rulers with their Hispano-Roman subjects. The Third Council of Toledo in 589 marked this momentous transition, symbolizing the integration of the Visigothic rulers into the broader Roman Catholic tradition.

This religious unification had profound implications for the kingdom's cultural and political landscape. It brought greater cohesion within the diverse society of Hispania and aligned the Visigothic Kingdom more closely with the rest of Christian Europe. The Church, gaining royal patronage, flourished during this period, becoming a vital institution in the cultural and political realms.

***

The Visigothic Kingdom's most significant and enduring contribution to the annals of law and governance was the *Liber Judiciorum*, later known as the Visigothic Code. This code, developed and refined over the 7th century, was groundbreaking in a world where legal systems were often fragmented and ethnically biased.

This legal code represented a synthesis of Roman legal traditions and Germanic customs, a harmonization effort that was ambitious and innovative for its time. The Romans had left behind a rich legacy of jurisprudence characterized by sophisticated legal theories and practices. The Germanic tribes, including the Visigoths, brought their customs and laws, which were largely unwritten and based on tribal traditions.

The Visigothic Code sought to bridge these two systems. It attempted to create a unified legal framework that could govern the diverse population of Hispania - a mix of the Romanized populace and the Germanic settlers. This unification of law was a significant step towards social and political stability in the kingdom, as it provided a standard set of rules and regulations for all subjects, regardless of their ethnic background.

The code was comprehensive, covering a wide range of legal areas. It included laws on property rights, inheritance, contracts, family law, and criminal justice. The laws were detailed and specific, providing clear guidelines for daily life and societal interactions.

One of the notable aspects of the Visigothic Code was its approach to justice and penalties. The code aimed to move away from the traditional Germanic practice of blood revenge and feuds, promoting a system where disputes could be settled legally. Rather than corporal punishment or revenge, Fines were often prescribed for offenses, indicating a shift towards a more regulated and orderly approach to justice.

The code also addressed the rights and duties of different classes of society, including the nobility, clergy, freemen, and slaves. It laid out regulations for commerce and trade, reflecting the growing complexity of economic life in the kingdom.

The Visigothic Code was not just significant for its immediate impact in Hispania. Its influence extended beyond the borders of the Visigothic Kingdom and the era of Visigothic rule. After the Islamic conquest of Hispania, the code continued to be used in the Christian territories of northern Spain, influencing the development of medieval Spanish law.

The code's attempt to create a unified legal system for a diverse population was a concept ahead of its time. It demonstrated an understanding of the need for a common legal framework to foster stability and unity within a multicultural and multiethnic society.

The legal framework established by the Visigothic Kingdom was a remarkable achievement in the medieval world. It represented a fusion of Roman and Germanic legal principles and an effort to create a cohesive and stable society through a unified code of law. The legacy of the Visigothic Code is a testament to the kingdom's contribution to the evolution of legal systems in Europe. This legacy endured well beyond the Visigoths' reign in Hispania.

SEEDS OF DISSENT

The Visigothic Kingdom, though outwardly unified under the banner of Catholicism after the conversion of the Visigothic elite, was not devoid of religious strife. One of the most significant sources of tension was the treatment of Jews within the kingdom. The Jews, who had been a part of Hispania since Roman times, found themselves increasingly marginalized and persecuted under Visigothic rule, especially in the later years of the kingdom.

These tensions were exacerbated by a series of laws that aimed to curtail Jewish religious practices and force conversions to Christianity. The Visigothic rulers, influenced by the Church, viewed the Jewish faith as a challenge to the religious and social order of the kingdom. This persecution created a divide within the society and destabilized the kingdom, as it alienated a significant portion of the population and led to internal unrest.

Another source of dissent lay in the relationship between the nobility and the monarchy. While possessing considerable authority, the Visigothic kings were often challenged by the powerful noble families. These nobles, comprising Visigothic and Hispano-Roman elites, held significant sway over regional territories and commanded their military forces.

The nobility's power was a double-edged sword for the monarchy. On the one hand, noble support was crucial for maintaining control over the widespread and diverse kingdom. On the other hand, ambitious and powerful nobles could become rivals to the king, leading to power struggles and even civil wars. These internal conflicts within the ruling class weakened the kingdom's cohesion and diverted attention from external threats.

The Visigothic Kingdom comprised several ethnic groups, including the Visigoths, Hispano-Romans, other Germanic tribes, and a sizable Jewish community. Integrating these diverse peoples into a cohesive society was a persistent challenge.

While the *Liber Judiciorum* represented an effort to create a unified legal framework for all inhabitants of the kingdom, cultural and ethnic differences remained. The Germanic customs of the Visigoths often clashed with the Romanized ways of the Hispano-Romans. This cultural divide was further complicated by the presence of other groups, each with their traditions and practices.

These differences were cultural and manifested in economic and social disparities. The distribution of land and wealth, the administration of justice, and access to political power were all areas where ethnic and cultural divisions were evident. These disparities often led to social tensions and unrest, undermining the kingdom's stability.

***

As the 8th century approached, the Visigothic Kingdom navigated a period of significant turmoil and vulnerability. The internal strife that had plagued the kingdom for years – the religious conflicts, the struggles between the nobility and the monarchy, and the challenges of integrating a diverse populace – had taken a toll on the stability and strength of the realm.

This period was marked not only by domestic challenges but also by external pressures. The kingdom's borders were not immune to the ambitions of neighboring powers, and the Visigoths had to defend their territory against external threats constantly. These continuous conflicts strained the kingdom's resources and further exacerbated the internal divisions.

The monarchy, which should have been a unifying force, was weakened by succession disputes and power struggles within the royal family. The kingship, often changing hands through intrigue and violence, had lost the stability and continuity needed to govern a diverse and widespread kingdom effectively.

The nobility, wielding considerable power in their own right, were often more focused on their regional interests and personal ambitions than on the collective well-being of the kingdom. This fragmentation of power among the nobility further weakened the central authority and undermined efforts to present a united front against external threats.

The kingdom's social fabric was also under strain. The persecution of Jews and the ongoing efforts to integrate various ethnic and cultural groups had created a society marked by tension and mistrust. These internal divisions weakened the kingdom socially and left it vulnerable to external incursions, as there was a lack of cohesive national identity or unity.

Externally, the Visigothic Kingdom faced a growing threat from the Islamic world. Having established a strong presence in North Africa, the Umayyad Caliphate was looking across the Strait of Gibraltar with expansionist eyes. The Islamic forces, buoyed by their recent successes in North Africa, were poised to take advantage of the disarray within the Visigoths on the Iberian Peninsula, serving as a bridge between Europe and Africa, made it an attractive target for the expanding Umayyad Caliphate. The political instability and weakened military capacity of the Visigothic Kingdom presented an opportune moment for invasion.

On the eve of the Umayyad conquest, the Visigothic Kingdom was a realm shadowed by uncertainty and decline. The cumulative effect of years of internal discord had left the kingdom ill-prepared to face a formidable external adversary. The societal rifts, the lack of a strong central leadership, and the depleted military resources were critical vulnerabilities that an invading force could exploit.

The Islamic forces, under the command of Tariq ibn Ziyad, recognized these weaknesses. As they gathered across the Strait of Gibraltar, preparing for their incursion, the fate of the Visigothic Kingdom hung in the balance. The impending clash was not merely a confrontation of armies but a collision of cultures, religions, and empires.

The Umayyad crossing of the Strait of Gibraltar in 711 marked the beginning of a new era in the history of the Iberian Peninsula. The ensuing battles, most notably the Battle of Guadalete, would not only decide the fate of the Visigothic Kingdom but also reshape the cultural and political landscape of the region for centuries to come.

With its blend of Roman legacy and Germanic traditions, the Visigothic Kingdom stood on the brink of a monumental shift. The arrival of the Umayyads was a catalyst that would transform the Iberian Peninsula, ushering in a period of Islamic rule and setting the stage for al-Andalus's complex and multifaceted history.

In this prelude to conquest, the stage was set for one of the most significant turning points in European and Islamic history. The fall of the Visigothic Kingdom and the rise of Islamic rule in Hispania would change the course of the Iberian Peninsula and have far-reaching effects on the broader history of the medieval world.

ERA OF LEOVIGILD

Our journey through the history of Visigothic Hispania brings us to one of its most influential rulers: King Leovigild. Ascending to the throne in 568, Leovigild's reign was a defining period in consolidating the Visigothic Kingdom. He was a ruler of both vision and pragmatism, understanding the complexities of governing a diverse realm.

Leovigild embarked on campaigns to subdue the independent regions within the peninsula, bringing territories like the Suevic Kingdom in the northwest under Visigothic control. His military campaigns were not merely conquests but strategic moves to unify the kingdom under a central authority.

But Leovigild's vision extended beyond the battlefield. He reformed the legal and administrative systems, integrating Roman traditions with Visigothic laws. These reforms aimed to create a more cohesive state that could accommodate its people's diversity.

His efforts to standardize coinage and promote trade were steps towards economic stability and prosperity.

Leovigild's successor, his son Reccared, took the throne in a kingdom primed for significant change. Reccared's reign is most remembered for a pivotal event in the history of the Visigothic Kingdom: the conversion of the Visigothic elite from Arianism to Catholic Christianity.

This conversion, announced at the Third Council of Toledo in 589, was more than a religious shift; it was a strategic move to unify the kingdom under a single religious creed. The Arianism faith, which had set the Visigothic rulers apart from their Hispano-Roman subjects, was replaced by Catholicism prevalent among the populace. This alignment with the Catholic Church bridged a significant divide between the Goths and Romans and strengthened the monarchy's position by gaining the support of the influential Catholic clergy.

The significance of Reccared's conversion cannot be overstated. It marked the beginning of a new era in the Visigothic Kingdom, where religious unity bolstered the political and social cohesion of the realm.

The Councils of Toledo, particularly during the reigns of Leovigild and Reccared, were instrumental in shaping the governance and social structure of the kingdom. These councils, attended by bishops and nobles, were forums where matters of state, law, and religion were discussed and decreed.

The decrees issued at these councils reflected the efforts to integrate the diverse elements of Visigothic society. They addressed issues ranging from succession laws and land rights to religious practices and social customs. The Councils of Toledo were a testament to the kingdom's attempts to govern a complex and multi-ethnic society through a blend of dialogue, law, and religious influence.

The reigns of Leovigild and Reccared and the significant events of their times were pivotal in forming the Visigothic Kingdom. Leovigild's campaigns and administrative reforms laid the groundwork for a unified state, while Reccared's religious conversion brought about a crucial societal alignment.

***

Following the transformative reigns of Leovigild and Reccared, the Visigothic Kingdom continued its journey through history, albeit with increasing challenges. The shifts initiated by these rulers set in motion a series of events that would test the resilience of the kingdom.

While unifying in many aspects, the kingdom's integration under Catholic Christianity did not entirely quell religious and social tensions. For instance, the kingdom's Jewish population found themselves under increasing pressure, leading to social unrest that further complicated the kingdom's internal dynamics.

Moreover, the newfound religious unity did not entirely erase the cultural and political divides between the Visigothic and Hispano-Roman populations. These lingering divisions, coupled with the ambitions of powerful nobles, continued to challenge the kings' central authority.

The governance model established during the reigns of Leovigild and Reccared, particularly the role of the Councils of Toledo, had lasting impacts. While instrumental in shaping laws and policies, these councils also reflected the ongoing power struggle between the monarchy, the nobility, and the Church. The delicate balance of power among these groups was a constant thread in the kingdom's narrative, influencing its stability and policies.

The Visigothic legal reforms, especially those about succession, land rights, and the administration of justice, had far-reaching effects. These reforms laid the groundwork for a legal system that would endure beyond the Visigothic era, influencing subsequent legal traditions in the Iberian Peninsula.

Externally, the Visigothic Kingdom faced pressures from neighboring realms and emerging powers. These external threats, combined with the internal fissures, tested the kingdom's military and diplomatic mettle. The Visigoths, renowned for their warrior heritage, had to continually adapt their strategies to protect their borders and maintain their sovereignty.

Despite these challenges, the Visigothic Kingdom demonstrated remarkable resilience. It survived internal upheavals, religious transformations, and external invasions, maintaining its identity and sovereignty for centuries.

As the Visigothic Kingdom navigated through these trials and transformations, the stage was set for the Reconquista. The legacy of the Visigothic era, with its blend of cultures, legal traditions, and religious shifts, would significantly influence the events that unfolded in the centuries to come.

A Kingdom Divided

D elving deeper into the history of the Visigothic Kingdom, we encounter a period marked by growing fissures within the fabric of the realm. Internal weaknesses and external pressures began to unravel the once-sturdy Visigothic Hispania. Despite its outward appearance of strength and unity, the Visigothic Kingdom was beset by a series of internal challenges that eroded its foundations.

The Kingdom's reliance on its nobility was a fundamental aspect of its governance structure, yet this reliance was fraught with challenges. With their substantial landholdings, military support, and regional influence, the nobles were indispensable to the kingdom's administration and defense. However, the strength that made them valuable to the kingdom made them a constant source of internal conflict.

The ambitions of the Visigothic nobility often extended beyond serving the realm. Many nobles harbored aspirations for greater power and autonomy, aspirations that frequently led to conflicts with the monarchy and among themselves. These ambitions were not merely about personal power; they were intertwined with issues of land ownership, control over resources, and regional influence.

Noble rivalries often manifested in bids for greater autonomy. Powerful nobles, especially those ruling distant or strategically essential territories, sought to assert their independence from central authority. Such bids were a challenge to the king's authority and a threat to the kingdom's cohesion.

Kings often found themselves entangled in the complex web of noble intrigues, needing to balance the demands and loyalties of various factions. This balancing act was delicate and risky; favoring one faction could alienate others, leading to further divisions and even rebellion.

The frequent shifts in noble alliances and loyalties made it challenging for the monarchy to implement consistent policies and maintain stable governance. The kingdom's administration, reliant on the cooperation of these powerful nobles, was often disrupted by their disputes and power plays.

The noble disputes also led to regional divisions within the kingdom. Nobles, aligning themselves with local interests, often acted in ways that benefited their territories at the expense of national unity. Ethnic and cultural differences compounded these regional divisions, as many nobles identified more closely with their local constituencies than with the kingdom.

Political intrigue was a hallmark of this period. Noble families engaged in a constant game of maneuvering for power and influence. Alliances were made and broken, plots were hatched, and betrayals were not uncommon. This intrigue and instability environment further undermined the monarchy's authority and the kingdom's unity.

Unlike the hereditary systems of many contemporary kingdoms, the Visigothic method of succession was characterized by its relative fluidity. The Visigoths, rooted in Germanic traditions, often selected their kings from among the noble elite, a process involving powerful nobles' input and agreement. This approach, while democratic in theory, led to a volatile and often unpredictable path to the throne.

The selection of a king was a complex affair, heavily influenced by the ambitions and intrigues of the nobility. Powerful noble families sought to install candidates who would serve their interests, leading to intense politicking and maneuvering during times of succession. This involvement of the nobility in the selection process often meant that the candidate who ascended to the throne had the most support among the nobles rather than the most capable or popular leader.

The lack of a clear hereditary succession system led to frequent disputes and power struggles over the throne. Kingship in the Visigothic Kingdom was often contested, with rival claimants and their supporters vying for control. This instability at the top echelons of power resulted in a lack of continuity and stability in leadership, which had far-reaching consequences for the kingdom.

Each change in kingship brought about shifts in policies, allegiances, and priorities. The constant change in leadership hindered the development of a long-term vision for the kingdom and disrupted the continuity of governance. This situation was exacerbated by the fact that some reigns were cut short by assassinations or coups, events that were not uncommon in the volatile political climate of the time.

The succession crises had a detrimental impact on the monarchy's ability to project power and maintain order. Often seen as a figurehead of competing noble interests, the king struggled to assert strong central authority. The frequent challenges to the throne, whether from within the royal family or from powerful nobles, eroded the legitimacy and effectiveness of the monarchy.

The weakness of the monarchy in the face of noble power struggles also impacted the kingdom's military and diplomatic capabilities. Constantly securing and maintaining noble support diverted attention and resources from external threats and governance challenges. This situation left the kingdom vulnerable to both internal revolts and external incursions.

The succession crises in the Visigothic Kingdom significantly influenced its eventual decline. The lack of a stable, hereditary succession system led to a kingdom plagued by leadership disputes, undermining the strength and authority of the monarchy.

These crises were symptomatic of deeper issues within the Visigothic political system – issues that weakened the kingdom's fabric and set the stage for its vulnerability to the transformative events of the 8th century.

SOCIETY IN STRAIN

The Visigothic Kingdom was a melting pot where various peoples coexisted under the rule of the Visigoths. The cultural and religious diversity of the kingdom had the potential to be a source of strength, fostering a rich and varied society. However, more often than not, it manifested as a source of tension and conflict.

These groups' differing customs, languages, and religious practices created a complex societal landscape, one where harmonious coexistence was frequently challenged by underlying discord.

One of the primary rifts was between the Hispano-Romans and the ruling Visigoths. The Hispano-Romans, with their long-standing traditions and customs rooted in the Roman Empire, often found themselves at odds with the Germanic practices and laws of the Visigoths.

The Hispano-Romans, descendants of the Roman settlers and indigenous populations of the Iberian Peninsula, were deeply ingrained with the customs, traditions, and legal systems of the Roman Empire. Their way of life, language, and social structures continued the Roman legacy that had dominated the region for centuries.

In contrast, the Visigoths, originally a Germanic tribe from central and eastern Europe, brought different customs, legal concepts, and social structures. Their culture was shaped by their migratory history, interactions with other tribes, and their unique Germanic heritage.

Language played a significant role in highlighting and perpetuating the divide between the Hispano-Romans and the Visigoths. The Hispano-Romans spoke Latin, the language of administration, law, and literature in the Roman Empire. Latin was a means of communication and a symbol of Roman cultural and intellectual heritage.

The Visigoths, on the other hand, spoke various Germanic dialects, which reflected their tribal origins and migratory journey. Their language was a marker of their identity, distinguishing them from the Hispano-Roman population they governed. This linguistic divide was a constant reminder of the cultural differences between the two groups and often acted as a barrier to full integration.

The legal systems of the Hispano-Romans and the Visigoths were another area of divergence. The Roman legal tradition, with its sophisticated and well-established codes, contrasted with the Germanic legal practices of the Visigoths, which were largely customary and less formalized. This difference in legal traditions often led to disparities in the administration of justice and governance.

Socially, the divide was evident in marriage customs, inheritance laws, and property rights. The Visigothic elite, adhering to their customs, often conflicted with the expectations and practices of the Hispano-Roman populace.

The Christian Church played a complex role in this cultural landscape. Initially, the Visigoths adhered to Arian Christianity, while the Hispano-Romans were predominantly Catholic. The eventual conversion of the Visigoths to Catholicism under King Reccared did not immediately bridge the cultural divide. Still, it did provide a common religious framework that helped to mitigate some aspects of the discord.

The treatment of the Jewish community was a particularly contentious issue in the Visigothic Kingdom. The Jews had a long history in the Iberian Peninsula, dating back to Roman times and possibly earlier. Under Visigothic rule, particularly during later periods, they faced increasing persecution.

The kingdom's policies towards Jews shifted over time, often reflecting the current king's or the Church's stance. Measures ranged from forced conversions and bans on practicing Judaism to more extreme actions like expulsion and confiscation of property.

These policies not only caused suffering and upheaval within the Jewish community but also contributed to societal instability, as they were often met with resistance and fostered resentment.

Jews in Hispania, having established deep roots and contributed significantly to the cultural and economic fabric of the region, found themselves increasingly marginalized under Visigothic rule. The fluctuating policies towards Jews – ranging from tolerance to outright persecution – mirrored the kingdom's broader struggles with diversity and integration. The treatment of Jews became a barometer for the kingdom's societal health and tolerance.

Economic disparities also contributed to societal strains. The largely rural economy favored the landowning elites, often leaving the lower classes, including peasants and artisans, in a state of dependency and vulnerability. This economic imbalance was exacerbated by occasional famines and plagues, disproportionately affecting the poorer segments of society. Economic hardships often led to social unrest, further challenging the cohesion and stability of the kingdom.

The Visigothic military, a crucial instrument of state power, was also a reflection of the societal divisions. Comprising primarily of Visigothic warriors, the military was often seen as an extension of Visigothic dominance, contributing to other groups' alienation.

Despite these challenges, the Visigothic Kingdom also witnessed moments of cultural exchange and assimilation. Over time, elements of Visigothic and Hispano-Roman cultures began to intertwine, creating a unique blend that was neither entirely Roman nor Germanic. This cultural synthesis was evident in art, architecture, and even some aspects of law and governance.

The societal strains within the Visigothic Kingdom resulted from its diverse and complex makeup. The rifts between the Hispano-Romans and the Visigoths, the treatment of the Jewish community, economic disparities, and the role of the military and the Church all shaped the kingdom's internal dynamics.

These strains, while challenging, also contributed to the rich and multifaceted Visigothic Kingdom, with its rich blend of cultures, religions, and social structures, poised between its legacy and the dawn of a new era in the Iberian Peninsula.

FRAGILE ECONOMY

The economic foundation of the Visigothic Kingdom was primarily agricultural. While agriculture was a vital sector, providing sustenance for the populace and wealth for the kingdom, its dominance also made the economy vulnerable.

The kingdom lacked significant diversification; other sectors like trade, industry, and mining were less developed or as robust as agriculture. This over-reliance on agriculture meant that any disruption in agricultural production – whether due to poor harvests, natural disasters, or warfare – had far-reaching consequences for the kingdom's economy and stability.

While present, trade in the Visigothic Kingdom was limited in scope and scale compared to the bustling trade networks of the Mediterranean world. The kingdom's relative isolation and the focus on a self-sufficient agricultural economy limited opportunities for extensive trade. This situation was further compounded by the lack of a strong maritime tradition, which restricted sea trade, and the kingdom's periodic conflicts with neighboring powers, which disrupted overland trade routes. The limited trade constrained economic growth and reduced the kingdom's access to foreign goods, innovations, and ideas.

Maintaining a large and effective military presence was essential for the Visigothic Kingdom, given its constant need to defend against external threats and to manage internal strife. However, sustaining such a military force was a significant financial burden. The costs associated with maintaining armies, fortifications, and military equipment strained the kingdom's treasury. This burden was cumbersome during war or when the kingdom embarked on military campaigns to expand or consolidate its territory.

Like much of the medieval world, the Visigothic Kingdom was periodically afflicted by famines and plagues. These natural calamities had a devastating impact on the kingdom's economy and society. Famines led to food shortages, skyrocketing prices, and widespread suffering, particularly among the peasantry and the poor. Plagues decimated populations, disrupted labor forces and caused social and economic upheaval. The kingdom's over-reliance on agriculture made these famines all the more crippling, as the loss of crops directly translated into a crisis for the entire economy.

These economic pressures – the over-reliance on agriculture, limited trade, the burden of military expenditures, and the impact of famines and plagues – cumulatively strained the kingdom's resources. The economic challenges limited the monarchy's ability to govern effectively and respond to internal and external threats.

They also contributed to social unrest, as economic hardships often led to increased discontent among the populace.

The Visigothic Kingdom's heavy reliance on a rural, agrarian-based economy was a critical vulnerability. Agriculture, while the backbone of the economy, was subject to the whims of nature. Unpredictable weather patterns, such as droughts or excessive rains, could drastically affect crop yields. This dependence on agriculture made the kingdom susceptible to food shortages and economic instability, exacerbated by the limited infrastructure for storing and distributing agricultural produce.

The Visigothic Kingdom exhibited a noticeable lack of industrial development compared to other contemporary societies. There was minimal investment in industries that could diversify the economy and provide alternative sources of income and employment. Crafts and artisanal trades existed but on a small scale, insufficient to significantly bolster the economy. The lack of industrialization meant the kingdom could not fully exploit its natural resources, such as minerals, which could have provided additional wealth and trade opportunities.

The Visigothic Kingdom also suffered from inadequate infrastructure, particularly transportation and communication. The Roman roads, once the arteries of commerce and communication across Hispania, were in decline, not receiving the maintenance and investment they required. This deterioration hampered both domestic trade and integration of the kingdom's diverse regions, further contributing to economic inefficiencies and regional disparities.

The kingdom's financial management, particularly in taxation and revenue collection, was another area of concern. The taxation system was often arbitrary and lacked uniformity, leading to inefficiencies and the potential for corruption. The burden of taxation fell unevenly across the populace, sometimes exacerbating social tensions. Moreover, the kingdom's revenue was often insufficient to cover its expenditures, particularly during times of war, leading to financial strains.

The economic strains of the kingdom had tangible social impacts. The peasantry, who formed the majority of the population, bore the brunt of these economic challenges. Their livelihoods, tied closely to the land and the vagaries of agricultural production, were fragile. Social unrest, borne out of economic hardship, was a recurring problem, sometimes manifesting in local rebellions or banditry, further destabilizing the kingdom.

The limited trade of the Visigothic Kingdom also meant a reliance on foreign goods for certain commodities, which could lead to trade imbalances. The kingdom was a net importer of luxury goods and necessities, which it had to pay for with its limited exports, primarily agricultural products. While necessary, this reliance on foreign trade placed the kingdom in a vulnerable economic position.

The economic foundation of the Visigothic Kingdom was marked by significant vulnerabilities: an over-reliance on agriculture, a lack of industrial and infrastructural development, inadequate financial management, and limited trade capabilities.

These economic challenges, intertwined with the kingdom's political, social, and military issues, created a scenario of compounded vulnerabilities. These economic strains emerged as pivotal factors contributing to the kingdom's inability to withstand the pressures that ultimately led to its downfall and the onset of a new era in the Iberian Peninsula.

An Unsettled Frontier

One of the significant external pressures on the Visigothic Kingdom came from the Eastern Roman (Byzantine) Empire. The Byzantines, having established a foothold in the southern part of the Iberian Peninsula during the latter stages of the Roman Empire, continued to maintain their presence in the region known as Spania. Though diminished from its peak, this Byzantine territory was a constant source of friction and a reminder of the Visigothic Kingdom's incomplete dominion over Hispania.

The Byzantine provinces in Hispania were not just passive remnants of a once-greater empire. They were actively maintained and often served as bases for Byzantine ambitions in the region. The Byzantine rulers, viewing themselves as the true heirs of the Roman Empire, sought to preserve and possibly expand their influence in Hispania.

The Byzantine presence posed several challenges to the Visigothic Kingdom. Militarily, the Byzantines were a formidable force, with well-trained armies and a strong naval presence in the Mediterranean. This military strength meant that the Visigoths had to maintain a vigilant defense along their southern borders, diverting resources and attention from other pressing issues within the kingdom.

Diplomatically, the Byzantine territories in Hispania were a complicating factor in the Visigothic Kingdom's foreign relations. The Byzantines, with their extensive network of alliances and influence, could potentially rally support against Visigothic interests. The existence of a foreign power within the peninsula also provided a potential refuge and a rallying point for dissidents and rebels within the Visigothic Kingdom.

The Byzantine presence in southern Hispania also had economic and cultural implications. The Byzantine territories were often more prosperous and better organized, with access to the wider Mediterranean trade networks. This contrast highlighted the economic challenges faced by the Visigothic Kingdom and may have fueled discontent among the populace in border regions.

Culturally, the Byzantines represented a continuation of the Roman legacy in Hispania, a legacy that was both admired and resented. The Byzantine provinces, with their adherence to Roman law, traditions, and Orthodox Christianity, were a constant reminder of the peninsula's diverse cultural and religious landscape.

The ongoing presence of the Byzantine Empire in Hispania was a thorn in the side of the Visigothic Kingdom. It represented a challenge to the kingdom's claims of sovereignty over the entire peninsula and a constant reminder of the competitive and precarious nature of international politics in the early medieval period.

***

To the north of the Visigothic Kingdom, the growing power of the Frankish Kingdoms under the Merovingian and later Carolingian dynasties posed a significant external threat. This expanding Frankish power, marked by military prowess and territorial ambitions, was a constant source of pressure and concern for the Visigothic rulers.

One of the most notable figures in this period was King Clovis, the founder of the Merovingian dynasty. Clovis, renowned for his military acumen and expansionist policies, led several campaigns encroaching upon Visigothic territories. His conquests, which extended Frankish rule over large parts of Gaul, were marked by strategic brilliance and a determination to expand his realm.

Clovis's victories were not just about territorial gains; they also had religious and cultural implications. His conversion to Catholic Christianity and his role in establishing the Catholic Church as a dominant force in his kingdom contrasted with the Arian Christianity of the Visigoths. This religious difference added another layer of complexity to the Frankish-Visigothic relations.

The Frankish expansion directly threatened the Visigothic Kingdom's northern borders. Regions once part of the Visigothic realm, particularly those in Gaul, came under Frankish control. These incursions represented a loss of territory and a strategic challenge, as they placed the Frankish forces in a position to exert influence and potentially launch further invasions into Visigothic lands.

The Visigothic Kingdom, already grappling with internal issues and the threat from the Byzantine south, had to contend with the reality of a powerful, aggressive neighbor to the north. The need to defend against Frankish incursions stretched the Visigothic military resources and added to the kingdom's strategic dilemmas.

In response to the Frankish threat, the Visigothic Kingdom engaged in a mix of diplomatic maneuvers and military preparations. Alliances were sought with other powers to counterbalance the Frankish influence, and efforts were made to fortify and defend vulnerable regions along the northern frontier.

Despite these efforts, the kingdom's responses were often hampered by its internal challenges and the fluctuating strength of its military. The kingdom had to navigate a delicate balance of defending its borders, maintaining internal stability, and projecting power in a region increasingly dominated by the Franks.

As the Frankish Kingdoms grew in power and influence under the Merovingians and later the Carolingians, the dynamics between the Franks and the Visigoths continued to evolve, marked by periods of conflict and uneasy peace. The expansionist policies of the Frankish rulers often brought them into direct confrontation with the Visigoths, particularly in regions that held strategic or economic significance.

A pivotal moment in the Frankish-Visigothic conflict was the Battle of Vouillé in 507, where King Clovis and his Frankish forces defeated the Visigoths led by King Alaric II. This battle, a landmark event in the history of Western Europe, significantly altered the balance of power in the region. The defeat at Vouillé resulted in the loss of the Visigothic control over much of Gaul, confining their dominion primarily to the Iberian Peninsula. The loss of these territories was a major blow to the Visigothic Kingdom, both strategically and psychologically.

Later, under the Carolingian dynasty, the pressure on the Visigothic Kingdom intensified. The Carolingians, particularly under Charlemagne, began military campaigns and expansionist policies threatening the Visigothic territories. The establishment of the Spanish March, a buffer zone between the Frankish Empire and the Muslim territories in Iberia, by Charlemagne, clearly indicated the Frankish intent to exert influence in the region.

The Visigothic Kingdom's response to these threats was often constrained by its internal struggles. The kingdom's focus on dealing with internal dissent, succession crises, and economic challenges meant its ability to counter the Frankish advances was limited. The necessity to defend against multiple fronts – dealing with the Byzantines in the south and the Franks in the north – significantly strained the kingdom's resources and military capabilities.

In the face of these challenges, the Visigothic rulers also turned to diplomacy to counter Frankish aggression. Alliances with neighboring powers, including sometimes with the Byzantine Empire or local Muslim rulers, were part of the Visigothic strategy to balance against Frankish expansion. These alliances, however, were often fragile and influenced by the shifting political landscape of the period.

The challenges posed by the Frankish threat and the kingdom's internal vulnerabilities created a scenario where the Visigothic Kingdom was constantly under pressure. This backdrop of external aggression and internal turmoil set the stage for the eventual decline of Visigothic power in the Iberian Peninsula, paving the way for the dramatic changes that would usher in the era of the Reconquista.

EMPIRE AT THE GATES

Across the narrow waters of the Strait of Gibraltar, the Visigothic Kingdom faced an emerging and formidable adversary: the Umayyad Caliphate. Having established a dominant Islamic empire that stretched from the Middle East to North Africa, the Umayyads represented a new and potent force in the Mediterranean world. Their expansion into North Africa, marked by military prowess and effective governance, brought them to the very doorstep of the Iberian Peninsula.

The Umayyad expansion was driven by religious zeal and territorial ambition. The Islamic conquests, initially sparked by the teachings and success of Prophet Muhammad, had transformed into a powerful movement for spreading Islam and establishing a vast empire under the Umayyad Caliphate. The Caliphate's leaders saw the expansion into new territories as a political and military objective and a religious duty to spread the Islamic faith.

The politically fractured landscape of Hispania presented an attractive target for the Umayyads. The Visigothic Kingdom, weakened by internal dissent, succession crises, and economic strains, appeared vulnerable to an external invasion. Additionally, the religious and social unrest within the kingdom, particularly the discontent among the Jewish and other non-Catholic communities, created potential opportunities for the Umayyads to exploit.

The Umayyads, observing the situation in Hispania, saw a chance to extend their empire into Europe. Adding the rich and fertile lands of the Iberian Peninsula to their realm was a tempting prospect. Furthermore, the conquest of Hispania was seen not just as a territorial gain but also as a stepping stone for further expansions into the heart of Europe.

The Strait of Gibraltar was a strategic gateway between North Africa and the Iberian Peninsula. Control of this narrow passage was crucial for any military campaign from Africa into Europe. Having established their dominance in North Africa, the Umayyads were in a prime position to launch an invasion across the strait. Their control of this critical maritime route allowed them to mobilize forces rapidly and launch incursions into Visigothic territory.

As the 8th century dawned, the stage was set for a dramatic encounter between the Umayyad Caliphate and the Visigothic Kingdom. The Umayyad preparations for an invasion of Hispania were not just a military campaign but a culmination of their broader ambitions and religious objectives.

The Caliphate, known for its sophisticated military tactics and diplomatic acumen, carefully assessed the political and social landscape of the Visigothic Kingdom. They recognized the potential for alliances with discontented factions within Hispania, which could be leveraged to facilitate their conquest.

The Umayyad expansion into the Visigothic Kingdom was a crucial factor in the shifting fortunes of the Iberian Peninsula. The combination of the Umayyads' strategic planning, military might, and the internal weaknesses of the Visigothic Kingdom culminated in a dramatic power shift. This period marked the end of Visigothic rule and the beginning of a significant new chapter in the history of Hispania, setting the stage for the centuries-long interaction between Islamic and Christian civilizations. This interaction would shape the region's destiny and resonate through the ages.

THE UMAYYAD CONQUEST

As the first light of dawn touched the shores of the Iberian Peninsula in the early 8th century, a storm was brewing across the narrow Strait of Gibraltar. This was no ordinary tempest but a storm of war and conquest that would forever alter the course of history. From the south, the Umayyad Caliphate, a burgeoning power in North Africa, set its sights on the fractured lands of the Visigothic Kingdom.

The figure at the heart of this impending invasion was Tariq ibn Ziyad, a commander whose name would become etched in the annals of history. Chosen by the Umayyad governor of North Africa for this ambitious endeavor, Tariq was not only a skilled general but also a visionary leader, driven by a blend of religious fervor and strategic insight.

In 711, Tariq gathered a formidable force, a mix of seasoned warriors and eager recruits, united under the banner of Islam.

Their objective was clear – to cross the Strait of Gibraltar and lay claim to the lands of Hispania.

Crossing the Strait of Gibraltar was a strategic gamble, a daring move that would set the tone for the entire campaign. Tariq's army, laden with weapons, horses, and the resolve of conquest, embarked on the journey across the strait. While not vast in distance, the narrow waterway represented a significant psychological barrier, marking the boundary between two worlds – the Islamic empire of the Umayyads and the Christian lands of the Visigothic Kingdom.

Upon landing on the shores of Hispania, at a point that would later bear Tariq's name – Jabal Tariq (Gibraltar), Tariq's forces quickly moved inland. Their arrival shocked the Visigothic Kingdom, unprepared for such a swift and bold incursion.

Tariq, capitalizing on the surprise and the disarray among the Visigoths, pushed his forces forward. The towns and fortresses that dotted the landscape fell in quickly as the Umayyad army swept through the territory.

As the Umayyad forces under Tariq ibn Ziyad made their way into the heart of the Visigothic Kingdom, tensions escalated to a fever pitch. Aware of the looming threat, King Roderic rallied his forces to confront the invaders. The stage was set for a confrontation that would not only decide the fate of a kingdom but also alter the course of history in the Iberian Peninsula.

The battle of Guadalete saw the clashing of two worlds: the Visigothic forces, representing the legacy of a fading empire, and the Umayyad army, the vanguard of a burgeoning Islamic expansion. King Roderic's army, composed of Visigothic warriors and levies from various regions of the kingdom, faced a well-organized and motivated Umayyad force.

Tariq had a deep understanding of his enemy's terrain and dynamics. He employed a combination of direct assaults and tactical maneuvers that exploited the weaknesses in the Visigothic battle lines. The Umayyad forces, adept in the art of warfare and bolstered by their belief in the righteousness of their cause, fought with a discipline and fervor that overwhelmed the defenders.

King Roderic led his troops into battle with bravery and determination. However, the Visigothic forces were plagued by internal divisions and a lack of unified command. The absence of a cohesive strategy and the inability to adapt to the changing dynamics of the battlefield proved to be their undoing. As the battle raged, the Visigothic lines crumbled under the relentless Umayyad assault.

The battle reached its climax with the fall of King Roderic. The death of the king was a devastating blow to the Visigothic morale. It symbolized the disintegration of the army and the very essence of Visigothic power. With their leader gone, the remnants of the Visigothic forces were thrown into disarray, and the battle was lost.

The aftermath of the Battle of Guadalete was grim for the Visigothic Kingdom. The defeat shattered the Visigothic military might and left the kingdom vulnerable to further incursions. The power vacuum created by the demise of King Roderic led to chaos and confusion, with no capable leader to rally the kingdom and mount a coherent defense.

The victory at Guadalete was a crucial milestone for the Umayyad campaign. It paved the way for their rapid advance throughout the peninsula. City after city fell to the conquering forces as the remnants of Visigothic resistance were either vanquished or assimilated.

The Battle of Guadalete was more than just a decisive military engagement; it was a historical turning point. The defeat of the Visigothic forces marked the end of an era and the beginning of a new chapter in the history of the Iberian Peninsula.

In the wake of Guadalete, the Umayyad forces continued their conquest of Hispania. City after city, region after region, fell to Tariq and his successors. The speed and effectiveness of the Umayyad campaign were a testament to their military capabilities and the strategic vulnerabilities of the Visigothic Kingdom.

The Umayyad conquest of Hispania was more than a mere change of rulers; it was a transformation of the very fabric of the peninsula. The arrival of Islamic culture, administration, and religion marked the beginning of a new era that would profoundly influence the region's history, culture, and identity.

The Umayyad storm from the south, rule, and the beginning of a period of Islamic dominance shaped the destiny of the peninsula for centuries to come.

THE FALL OF TOLEDO

Following the decisive victory at the Battle of Guadalete, the Umayyad forces, emboldened and strategic, turned their attention to Toledo, the heart of the Visigothic Kingdom. Toledo was not just a city but a symbol of Visigothic power and legacy, a bastion that held immense political and cultural significance. The siege of Toledo was a calculated move by the Umayyad conquerors aimed at striking at the core of Visigothic authority.

As the Umayyad forces laid siege to the city, the inhabitants of Toledo faced a dire situation. Encircled and under constant pressure, the city was a microcosm of the disintegrating Visigothic Kingdom. The defenses of Toledo, manned by soldiers and citizens alike, put up a brave resistance. However, the tide of the Umayyad conquest and the internal strife that plagued the kingdom had weakened Toledo's ability to withstand a prolonged siege.

The eventual fall of Toledo to the Umayyad forces was a moment of profound significance. The city's capture was not just a military victory but a symbolic act that signaled the end of the Visigothic reign in Hispania. Once the seat of Visigothic kings and a center of Christian authority, Toledo now lay in the hands of a new power.

The conquerors swiftly consolidated their hold over the region with Toledo under Umayyad control. The city's fall had a domino effect, leading to the rapid capitulation of neighboring areas. The Umayyad strategy relied not solely on military might but also on astute diplomatic maneuvers.

They offered terms that were often favorable to the local nobility and the populace, including assurances of religious freedom and protection of property rights, in exchange for loyalty and tribute. This approach facilitated the peaceful surrender of many towns and cities, thereby expanding Umayyad control with minimal resistance.

Under Umayyad rule, Toledo transformed from the capital of a Christian kingdom into a center of Islamic governance and culture. The city's strategic location and rich cultural heritage made it an ideal administrative and political center for the new rulers.

The Umayyads, recognizing the significance of Toledo, set about integrating the city into their broader administrative framework. They implemented new governance structures, blending Islamic principles with existing systems, to manage the diverse populace of the city and its surrounding regions.

The capture of Toledo also marked the beginning of significant cultural and religious changes. Islamic influence began to permeate the city, evident in its inhabitants' architecture, the arts, and daily life. Mosques were established, and Islamic scholars and artisans contributed to the city's intellectual and cultural landscape.

Despite these changes, Toledo retained elements of its Visigothic and Roman past. The Umayyads, known for their pragmatic approach to governance, often preserved and adapted existing structures and institutions.

The urban landscape evolved with the construction of mosques, public baths, and markets, showcasing the architectural prowess of Islamic artisans. The Visigothic structures were not entirely erased but were often repurposed, maintaining a connection to the city's past while embracing its new identity.

The Umayyad rule in Toledo heralded a period of cultural and intellectual flourishing. The city became a melting pot of ideas and traditions, where scholars, poets, and artists from diverse backgrounds gathered. The coexistence of Christians, Muslims, and Jews under the Umayyad administration led to a vibrant cultural exchange, fostering advancements in science, philosophy, and the arts. Toledo emerged as a beacon of learning, attracting intellectuals from the Islamic world and Europe.

One of the notable aspects of Umayyad rule in Toledo was the relative religious tolerance extended to Christians and Jews. While the Islamic rulers were firm in their authority, they generally allowed other religious communities to practice their faiths. This tolerance policy, though not without its limitations and instances of strife, contributed to Toledo's social stability and cultural richness.

The Umayyad conquest also brought about an economic revival in Toledo and its surrounding areas. Introducing new agricultural techniques, irrigation methods, and crops from the Islamic world transformed the agricultural landscape. Trade routes were reestablished and expanded, connecting Toledo to the broader economic networks of the Umayyad Empire and beyond.

The fall of Toledo to the Umayyads was more than a military conquest; it was a transformative event that reshaped the social, cultural, and economic contours of the city and the region. Toledo's story is a keen example of the profound changes wrought by the Umayyad conquest. It symbolizes the end of an era and the beginning of a new chapter in the history of the Iberian Peninsula, one marked by the intermingling of cultures, the flourishing of knowledge, and the emergence of a society that would leave a lasting legacy on the fabric of European and Islamic civilizations.

Adapting to New Realities

The Umayyad conquest of Hispania was not just a tale of military triumph; it was also a story of political astuteness and adaptability. Many localities within the Visigothic Kingdom, confronted with the reality of a rapidly changing political landscape, chose pragmatism over resistance. The internal divisions that had plagued the Visigothic Kingdom – between different factions of nobility, religious groups, and regional powers – created a situation where the allegiance of many local leaders was fluid and often opportunistic.

The Umayyads were adept at exploiting these divisions. They offered assurances to local leaders, promising respect for their customs, preservation of their rights, and religious freedoms. In many cases, these assurances were coupled with the promise of protection and stability under the Umayyad rule – a tempting proposition for regions that had experienced prolonged unrest and uncertainty.

The prospect of being part of the expansive and prosperous Umayyad Caliphate appealed to many localities. The Umayyads were known for their sophisticated governance systems, patronage of trade and culture, and relatively cosmopolitan approach to different faiths and cultures. This reputation and the tangible benefits of stability and economic opportunity made the transition to Umayyad rule more acceptable for many.

One of the economic incentives under the Umayyad administration was the revival and expansion of trade routes. With their extensive empire spanning from the Middle East to North Africa, the Umayyads brought Hispania into a vast trade network. This integration facilitated the flow of goods, ideas, and innovations across regions. Cities and towns along these trade routes flourished, becoming bustling centers of commerce and interaction. The influx of luxury goods from the East and everyday commodities enhanced the standard of living and provided new economic opportunities for local merchants and artisans.

Agriculture, the backbone of the Hispanian economy, saw significant advancements under the Umayyads. They introduced new crops, such as rice, cotton, and certain fruits, which were well-suited to the climate of the Iberian Peninsula. Moreover, the Umayyads brought sophisticated irrigation techniques, a legacy of their experience in arid regions, which led to increased agricultural productivity and expansion of cultivable land. These innovations improved food security and contributed to a more diversified and resilient agricultural sector.

The overall economic prosperity of the Umayyad Caliphate was a compelling factor for many in Hispania. The caliphate's wealth, accumulated through trade, taxation, and efficient administration, was evident in the cities they governed. This prosperity had a trickle-down effect, contributing to the economic vitality of the regions under Umayyad control. The promise of being part of this prosperous empire starkly contrasted with the economic struggles experienced under the late Visigothic Kingdom.

The Umayyad administration's approach to governance included stabilizing local economies. This stabilization was achieved through fair taxation policies, investment in infrastructure, and the establishment of marketplaces and trading posts. The Umayyads fostered an atmosphere conducive to growth and prosperity by providing a stable and predictable economic environment.

The Umayyad rule also appealed to the local elites, who saw economic benefits in aligning with the new rulers. The Umayyads often allowed local nobles and landowners to retain their properties and statuses, provided they paid allegiance to the new regime. This policy ensured the cooperation of the local elite, who played a crucial role in the economic life of their communities.

The Umayyad conquest led to a significant cultural exchange with direct economic implications. Fusing Islamic, Christian, and Jewish traditions under Umayyad rule fostered a climate of intellectual and technological exchange. This environment encouraged innovation in various fields, including agriculture, craftsmanship, and medicine, further stimulating economic development.

The revival of trade, agricultural advancements, and overall economic prosperity under the Umayyads not only enhanced the quality of life but also played a pivotal role in transforming the economic landscape of the Iberian Peninsula. This economic transformation underpinned the societal and cultural changes that followed, marking the Umayyad period as a time of significant progress and development in the history of Hispania.

Adapting to new realities under Umayyad rule in Hispania was a complex process influenced by a myriad of political, cultural, economic, and religious factors. The Umayyad conquest fundamentally altered the landscape of the Iberian Peninsula, not solely through military means but also a nuanced understanding of the local dynamics and a pragmatic approach to governance. This period of adaptation set the stage for a transformative era in Hispania, where old realities gave way to new possibilities, shaping the region's history in profound and enduring ways.

For the remnants of the Visigothic Kingdom, the Umayyad conquest marked the end of an era. However, the legacy of the Visigoths did not vanish entirely. Visigothic culture, law, and language elements persisted and intermingled with the new Islamic and Arabic influences. This blending of cultures would play a significant role in shaping the peninsula's future.

RESISTANCE IS FUTILE

In certain parts of the Iberian Peninsula, the arrival of the Umayyads was perceived as a liberation rather than a conquest. These regions, often marginalized or oppressed under Visigothic rule, found a chance for change and improvement in their circumstances in the Umayyad.

For example, areas with significant Jewish populations, which had faced persecution and discrimination under the Visigoths, saw the Umayyads as protectors who offered a more tolerant and inclusive rule. Similarly, other minority groups or regions that had been at odds with the central Visigothic authority due to political, cultural, or religious differences welcomed the Umayyad rule as an opportunity for greater autonomy and fairer treatment.

Conversely, the Umayyad conquest met with resistance in regions where Visigothic rule had been more stable, effective, or benevolent. These areas, often with strong ties to the Visigothic monarchy and its institutions, viewed the Umayyad invasion as a threat to their way of life and traditions. Resistance took various forms, from active military opposition to passive resistance, such as reluctance to adopt the new administrative and cultural changes introduced by the Umayyads.

The stance of local leaders significantly influenced the response to the Umayyad conquest. Local Visigothic or Hispano-Roman nobles sometimes collaborated with the Umayyads to retain their status and properties, facilitating the transition to Umayyad rule in their regions. In other cases, local leaders led the resistance against the Umayyads, rallying the population to defend their traditions and autonomy.

Even in areas that initially resisted, the Umayyad forces' overwhelming military superiority and Visigothic power's collapse often led to a begrudging acceptance of the new reality. Many communities realized resistance was futile and potentially disastrous, opting for a pragmatic adaptation to Umayyad rule. This adaptation was driven by a desire to preserve local interests, maintain social order, and avoid the devastation of warfare.

The economic and social policies of the Umayyads also played a role in garnering acceptance. The promise of economic stability, the opportunity for trade and prosperity under the Umayyad economic system, and the relative religious tolerance extended to Christians and Jews under Islamic rule swayed many to accept Umayyad governance.

Over time, the varied responses to the Umayyad rule contributed to the emergence of a diverse and multifaceted society. This society was characterized by a blend of cultures, religions, and traditions, shaped by the interactions and coexistence of Muslims, Christians, and Jews under Umayyad governance.

****

As the Umayyad rule extended over the peninsula, the initial varied responses gradually led to a more integrated society. This integration was facilitated by the Umayyads' policy of relative religious and cultural tolerance. While Islam became the dominant religion and Arabic the lingua franca, the Umayyads allowed Christians (known as Mozarabs) and Jews to maintain their religious practices and participate in the social and economic life of Al-Andalus. This inclusive approach fostered an environment where different communities could coexist, albeit within the framework of Islamic governance.

In areas where resistance to Umayyad rule had been strongest, a transformation occurred as communities adapted to the new political reality over time. The need for coexistence and the benefits of being part of a prosperous and stable empire led many to find ways to live under Umayyad rule while preserving their cultural identity.

The economic growth experienced under the Umayyads served as a unifying factor across the peninsula. Improved agricultural techniques, enhanced trade, and urban development under the Umayyads brought prosperity transcending cultural and religious boundaries. This prosperity contributed to shared interest and interdependence among the diverse communities.

Over the centuries of Umayyad rule, a distinct Andalusian identity emerged, blending elements of Islamic, Christian, and Jewish cultures. This new identity was characterized by a shared language (Arabic), common artistic and architectural styles, and a fusion of culinary and musical traditions. The legacy of this Andalusian identity would leave an indelible mark on the history and culture of the Iberian Peninsula.

The Umayyad conquest initially met with a spectrum of reactions and ultimately laid the foundation for a remarkable society for its diversity, intellectual vibrancy, and economic prosperity. This period illustrates the dynamic process of societal change and the formation of a unique and enduring legacy in the history of the Iberian Peninsula.

ESTABLISHMENT OF AL-ANDALUS

The Umayyad conquest led to the establishment of Al-Andalus, a rich and diverse region under Islamic rule. Al-Andalus became a melting pot of cultures, languages, and religions, where Muslims, Christians, and Jews coexisted and contributed to a vibrant and prosperous society. This period's architectural, scientific, and cultural achievements would leave a lasting legacy on the peninsula.

With the Umayyad conquest, a new political entity emerged, characterized by Islamic governance and a multicultural society. Al-Andalus, as this region came to be known, stretched across a vast portion of the peninsula and became a symbol of the Islamic Golden Age in Europe.

Its cultural diversity distinguished Al-Andalus. It was a place where Muslims, Christians (Mozarabs), and Jews lived side by side, contributing to the development of a society that was unique in its blend of traditions and perspectives. This multicultural environment was fostered by the Umayyads' policy of relative tolerance and their appreciation for the various cultures under their rule.

The architectural legacy of Al-Andalus is one of its most enduring contributions. Cities like Córdoba, Granada, and Seville were adorned with stunning architectural feats, combining Islamic artistry with Roman, Visigothic, and Byzantine influences. The Great Mosque of Córdoba, with its iconic arches and rich decoration, stands as a testament to the artistic and architectural prowess of the period. Similarly, the development of urban centers, with their bustling markets, public baths, and elaborate palaces, reflected the prosperity and sophistication of the period.

Significant scientific and intellectual achievements also marked Al-Andalus. Scholars in astronomy, medicine, mathematics, and philosophy thrived in this environment. The translation of ancient texts from Greek, Latin, and other languages into Arabic and later into the vernacular languages of Europe played a crucial role in preserving and disseminating knowledge. The works of scholars like Averroes (Ibn Rushd) and Maimonides, who were deeply influenced by the intellectual climate of Al-Andalus, had a profound impact on the Renaissance and the scientific revolution in Europe.

Culturally, Al-Andalus was a hub of artistic expression and innovation. Music, poetry, and literature flourished, often blending Arabic, Hebrew, and Romance elements. The convivencia (coexistence) of different religious and ethnic groups fostered a creative exchange that gave birth to new artistic forms and genres. This cultural synthesis was evident in the unique styles of Andalusian music, the ornamentation of manuscripts, and the evolution of a distinct poetic tradition.

Economically, Al-Andalus prospered due to its strategic position, fertile lands, and the Umayyads' emphasis on agricultural innovation. The introduction of new crops and irrigation techniques from the Islamic world transformed the agricultural landscape, increasing productivity and trade. Al-Andalus became a crucial player in the Mediterranean trade network, exporting textiles, ceramics, and agricultural products.

The impact of Al-Andalus extended into the realms of language and literature. Arabic, the official language of the Umayyads, became a lingua franca in the region, profoundly influencing the local Romance languages. This linguistic influence is evident in the many Arabic loanwords in Spanish and Portuguese today. Additionally, the cross-cultural interactions in Al-Andalus led to the development of Mozarabic, a Romance language influenced by Arabic.

The intermingling of Arabic, Hebrew, and Romance literary traditions gave rise to a rich body of poetry and prose characterized by themes of love, nature, and philosophical inquiry.

The artistic legacy of Al-Andalus is another significant aspect of its cultural influence. The intricate tilework, delicate calligraphy, and elaborate geometric patterns adorned buildings and objects are characteristic of Andalusian art. These artistic elements, which reflected a blend of Islamic and local artistic traditions, influenced the artistic development in the broader Mediterranean and European regions. Crafts such as ceramics, metalwork, and textiles from

Al-Andalus were highly prized and widely traded, showcasing the region's artistic and technical skills.

The intellectual and cultural achievements of Al-Andalus had a lasting impact on European thought and culture. The philosophical and scientific works produced in Al-Andalus and the translations of classical texts played a crucial role in the European Renaissance. The transmission of knowledge from Al-Andalus to the rest of Europe helped bridge the gap between the ancient world and the modern era. The scholarly exchanges in Al-Andalus shaped European philosophy, science, and medicine.

Al-Andalus was a center of cultural and intellectual activity in the Iberian Peninsula and a significant contributor to the broader Mediterranean and Islamic civilizations. Its strategic location made it a cultural and economic bridge between the Islamic world and Christian Europe. Al-Andalus served as a conduit for exchanging ideas, goods, and technologies between these two worlds, enhancing the cultural and intellectual landscapes.

The establishment of Al-Andalus under the Umayyad dynasty marked a period of unprecedented cultural, intellectual, and economic prosperity. Its legacy extends beyond the Umayyad rule, leaving an indelible mark on the Iberian Peninsula and Europe's history, culture, and languages.

TOLERANCE AND TAXATION

As the Umayyad banners unfurled over the Iberian Peninsula, marking the boundaries of a new realm, a profound religious transformation began. The establishment of Umayyad control heralded the introduction of Islam, a faith that would deeply interweave with the peninsula's religious tapestry.

In the early days of Umayyad rule, the conquerors approached the existing religious structures with a strategic tolerance. The Christian majority, along with the Jewish communities, were categorized as 'People of the Book' – a term used in Islam for communities with revealed scriptures.

This designation allowed them certain religious freedoms, albeit under the conditions of dhimmi status, which included paying the jizya tax, a form of tribute.

The imposition of the jizya was a double-edged sword. While it affirmed the right of non-Muslims to practice their faith, it also established a clear hierarchy in the new Islamic society. For many, paying the jizya was a practical alternative to conversion, allowing them to maintain their religious traditions. However, it also created a financial burden and a sense of subordination.

The spread of Islam in Hispania was not an overnight phenomenon but a gradual process. Conversion to Islam initially attracted certain population segments, particularly those seeking social and economic advantages in aligning with the new rulers. Over time, as the Umayyads solidified their control and the benefits of Muslim status became more pronounced, conversions increased.

The architectural landscape of Hispania began to reflect the religious changes. With their distinctive minarets and ornate mihrabs, Mosques rose in cities and towns, becoming centers of Islamic worship and community life. The Great Mosque of Córdoba, an architectural marvel, epitomized the grandeur of Islamic religious expression.

Some Christian communities viewed the Umayyad rule with apprehension. Others found ways to adapt, maintaining their faith while coexisting within the Islamic framework. The Mozarabs, Christians living under Muslim rule, developed a unique identity, blending their Christian traditions with Arab culture.

For the Jewish communities, the Umayyad conquest brought relative prosperity and freedom. Liberated from the restrictions of Visigothic rule, Jewish scholars, merchants, and artisans found opportunities for growth and intellectual pursuits. This era, often referred to as a 'Golden Age' for Hispano-Jewish culture, saw significant contributions to science, philosophy, and the arts.

The religious landscape of Al-Andalus became a fertile ground for interfaith dialogues and intellectual exchanges. Muslim, Christian, and Jewish scholars engaged in debates and collaborative works, exploring philosophy, theology, and science. This atmosphere of relative religious tolerance and intellectual curiosity was a hallmark of Umayyad Al-Andalus.

As the Umayyad rule entrenched itself in Hispania, Islamic jurisprudence and governance began to influence the legal and administrative systems of Al-Andalus. Sharia, the Islamic law, became the foundation of legal matters, influencing everything from commerce to personal conduct. The establishment of qadis (Islamic judges) and the application of Islamic principles in public and private life marked a significant shift in the legal landscape.

However, this integration was not a wholesale replacement but a layering of existing systems, creating a unique amalgam of Roman, Visigothic, and Islamic laws.

In the Islamic framework, the Caliph was a religious and political leader, embodying the unity of state and religion. This concept was new to the Christian and Jewish populations, accustomed to a separation of religious and royal authority. The Umayyads, while asserting their religious leadership in the Islamic context, had to navigate a complex interplay of religious authorities, balancing their role with that of Christian bishops and Jewish rabbis.

Islamic madrasas (schools) and libraries were established, attracting scholars from across the Muslim world. These institutions became centers for studying Islamic theology, law, and history. Similarly, Christian and Jewish communities in Al-Andalus experienced a renaissance of their scholarly traditions, often engaging in theological dialogues with their Muslim counterparts.

The religious practices and cultural expressions of the people of Al-Andalus evolved under the influence of Islamic rule. While Muslims, Christians, and Jews maintained their distinct religious identities, cultural practices were cross-pollinated. Religious festivals, culinary habits, and artistic expressions began to reflect a blend of influences, enriching the cultural fabric of Al-Andalus.

The religious transformation of Al-Andalus was not without its challenges and conflicts. Issues of religious conversions, non-Muslim status, and enforcing religious laws sometimes led to tensions and disputes. These challenges reflected the broader struggle to balance the ideals of religious tolerance with the realities of governing a diverse and multi-faith society.

The religious changes initiated by the Umayyad conquest of Hispania left an enduring impact on the region. The legacy of this era can be seen in the rich religious heritage, the architectural marvels, and the vast body of scholarly work that emerged from Al-Andalus. The interweaving of Islamic, Christian, and Jewish traditions created a unique tapestry that would influence the religious and cultural trajectory of the Iberian Peninsula for centuries to come.

The establishment of Umayyad control in Hispania and the resultant religious changes were pivotal in shaping the history of Al-Andalus. This era of confluence and interaction among different faiths created a society that, despite its challenges, was marked by a remarkable degree of religious diversity and intellectual vibrancy.

RISE OF A LEADER

As the dusk of the Visigothic Kingdom gave way to the dawn of Umayyad rule in Hispania, a figure emerged from the shadows of a crumbling empire – Pelayo. This name would resonate throughout history as a symbol of resistance and hope. His rise as a leader was set against a backdrop of conquest, cultural upheaval, and the search for identity in a land undergoing profound transformation.

Pelayo's early life was likely steeped in the martial traditions of the Visigoths. As a member of the nobility, he would have been trained in the art of warfare, a skill essential for survival and prestige in the Visigothic society. It is believed that Pelayo served as a soldier and possibly even ascended to the rank of a commander within the Visigothic army.

His military experience would have been crucial in shaping his leadership qualities and strategic cleverness, which later defined his resistance against the Umayyad conquest.

Within the courts of the Visigothic kings, Pelayo would have witnessed firsthand the complexities of governance and the fragility of power. This environment, rife with political maneuvering, could have given Pelayo insights into leadership and maintaining authority during adversity. The experiences gained at the court might have also instilled in him a sense of duty towards his kingdom and people, fueling his resolve to resist foreign domination.

As the Umayyad forces began their incursion into the Iberian Peninsula, the world as Pelayo knew it started to crumble. The rapid collapse of the Visigothic Kingdom under the onslaught of the Umayyad conquest would have been a pivotal moment in Pelayo's life. Witnessing the disintegration of his homeland and the retreat or capitulation of many of his contemporaries, Pelayo faced a defining choice – to flee, to submit, or to resist.

The decision to resist marked Pelayo's transformation from a soldier of a fading kingdom to a symbol of enduring defiance. His military background and noble status positioned him uniquely as a rallying point for those who yearned to reclaim their land and heritage. Pelayo's emergence as a leader of resistance was not just a response to the immediate circumstances but a culmination of his life's experiences, his noble lineage, and his intimate understanding of the warrior ethos of his people.

His defiance was not merely a reaction to the conquest but a stand for the sovereignty and traditions of his people. This bold and audacious rebellion quickly drew the attention of the Umayyad authorities, marking Pelayo as a threat to their control, leading to his capture by the Umayyads.

According to some historical accounts, he was taken prisoner and brought to Córdoba, the administrative and cultural epicenter of the Umayyad rule in Hispania. In Córdoba, Pelayo would have encountered the full might and sophistication of the Umayyad regime, a stark contrast to the crumbling Visigothic Kingdom he had known.

Córdoba, under the Umayyads, was a city of splendor and learning, far removed from the rugged landscapes of Asturias. Pelayo's imprisonment here was symbolic, representing the captivity of his homeland under foreign rule. However, rather than breaking his spirit, this experience is believed to have strengthened his resolve. While impressive, the diverse and vibrant culture of Córdoba also highlighted the loss of his people's independence and way of life.

Pelayo's time in captivity is shrouded in mystery, with various legends speaking of his daring escape. These tales, a blend of history and myth, describe Pelayo's audacious flight from Córdoba, eluding his captors and defying the odds. This escape was not just a physical journey but a symbolic act, representing the will of a leader destined to challenge the usurpers of his homeland.

Pelayo's return to the northern lands of Hispania was a journey fraught with danger and hardship. It was a trek through hostile territory, evading Umayyad patrols and seeking refuge with those still loyal to the Visigothic cause. This journey back to Asturias was a testament to Pelayo's resilience and determination, qualities that would define his leadership in the future.

The rugged mountains and deep valleys of Asturias in the north provided the perfect refuge for Pelayo and his followers. With its harsh terrain and resilient populace, this land was a natural fortress against the Umayyad forces. Here, amidst the untamed beauty of Asturias, Pelayo began to rally those who were dispossessed, disillusioned, or defiant against the Umayyad rule.

Pelayo's charisma and noble lineage made him a natural focal point for resistance. He gathered around him a motley band of warriors, locals, and remnants of the Visigothic army. These men and women were united by a common enemy and a shared sense of purpose – to reclaim their land and preserve their way of life.

Pelayo would be seen as more than a military leader; he symbolized hope and resistance. His struggle was not merely a fight against a conquering force but a stand for identity, faith, and independence. Pelayo's emergence as a leader marked the beginning of a long and arduous journey that would lay the foundations of the Reconquista and the reclamation of Hispania.

BATTLE OF COVADONGA

In the verdant valleys and rugged mountains of Asturias, a small band of warriors gathered, united under the banner of Pelayo, a nobleman whose defiance against the Umayyad conquerors had lit the flame of resistance. The Battle of Covadonga, set against this backdrop of defiance, was more than a military confrontation; it symbolized hope, a testament to the unyielding spirit of a people yearning for freedom.

As Pelayo and his followers prepared for battle, the Umayyad forces advanced towards Asturias, confident in their military superiority. Underestimating the resolve of Pelayo's band and the challenging terrain, the Umayyads anticipated an easy victory. But the Asturian mountains were a fortress in their own right, and Pelayo, well-versed in their nooks and crannies, planned to use this to his advantage.

Pelayo's strategy was one of guerrilla warfare, utilizing the natural defenses of the landscape. The narrow pass of Covadonga, where Pelayo chose to make his stand, was a perfect bottleneck to neutralize the numerical superiority of the Umayyad forces. Here, in the shadows of the mountains, Pelayo's men lay in wait, ready to strike.

The Battle of Covadonga was set in a rugged landscape that would play a decisive role in its outcome. The narrow pass, surrounded by steep cliffs and dense forests, was a natural fortress. With his intimate knowledge of this terrain, Pelayo chose this as the battleground, understanding its potential to neutralize the Umayyad numerical advantage.

The Umayyad troops, confident in their strength and previous victories across Hispania, advanced into the Asturian mountains, expecting little resistance from what they perceived as a ragtag group of rebels. However, as they marched into the pass of Covadonga, they found themselves not in open fields conducive to large-scale warfare but in a confined space that restricted their movement and formation.

Pelayo positioned his men strategically within the pass and the surrounding heights. The Asturians, though few, were prepared to use every advantage the landscape provided. They were not just fighting a military battle but defending their homeland, their families, and their way of life.

As the Umayyad forces maneuvered through the narrow pass, Pelayo and his warriors launched their attack. It was a sudden and ferocious assault that took the Umayyads by surprise. The Asturians, attacking from above and from hidden positions within the pass, unleashed a barrage of arrows, rocks, and spears. The

Umayyads, caught in the confined space, found it challenging to retaliate effectively and organize a counterattack.

The surprise attack caused chaos in the Umayyad ranks. The mountain pass, which had seemed like an easy route through the Asturian lands, turned into a death trap. The Umayyad cavalry, a key component of their military strength, was ineffective in the craggy terrain. The Asturians, meanwhile, continued their relentless assault, using their superior knowledge of the terrain to outmaneuver and outflank the invaders.

The battle reached its climax when the Umayyad troops, unable to sustain their formation and suffering heavy losses, began to retreat in disarray. The Asturians, sensing victory, pressed their advantage, driving the Umayyads out of the pass. The retreat quickly turned into a rout, with the Umayyad forces fleeing the battlefield, desperately trying to escape the Asturian onslaught.

The clash at Covadonga, though brief, was a defining moment in the Reconquista. This battle, where a small band of determined warriors triumphed against a formidable force, symbolized hope and resistance. The victory at Covadonga was a David versus Goliath moment, a small but resolute force triumphing against a seemingly invincible enemy.

The Umayyad retreat from Covadonga marked the first significant Christian victory in the Reconquista. While the battle's scale was modest, its impact resonated across the peninsula, igniting a spark that would grow into a centuries-long campaign to reclaim Hispania.

The aftermath of Covadonga saw Pelayo emerge not just as a military victor but as a symbol of Christian resistance against Islamic rule. Though tactically a minor skirmish, the battle had immense psychological and symbolic importance. It bolstered the morale of Christian communities across the peninsula and challenged the narrative of the inevitable spread of Umayyad rule.

The Battle of Covadonga is remembered as when the tide began to turn when the oppressed began to envision the possibility of liberation and the restoration of their lands. The battle became a rallying cry, a source of inspiration for future generations who took up the mantle of the Reconquista.

KINGDOM OF ASTURIAS

The echoes of the Battle of Covadonga reverberated through the valleys and peaks of Asturias, heralding the birth of a new Christian power in the northern fringes of the Iberian Peninsula. The victory, though modest in military terms, had immense symbolic significance. It was not merely a battle won; it was the awakening of a resistance, the genesis of what would become the Asturian Kingdom.

In the wake of Covadonga, Pelayo's stature rose dramatically. From being a leader of a band of rebels, he became a figurehead of Christian resistance and, eventually, a monarch. The local populace, galvanized by the victory and yearning for stability, rallied around Pelayo, seeing in him not just a military leader but a symbol of their aspirations for self-rule and preservation of their Christian heritage.

Pelayo, seizing the moment, began consolidating power in the region. He established his capital in Cangas de Onís, a strategic location that offered natural defense. From this stronghold, Pelayo and his successors embarked on a dual mission: fortifying their territorial holdings and forging a sense of Asturian identity, distinct from the Visigothic legacy and the Umayyad rule.

Pelayo embarked on this task with a vision to create a militarily resilient and administratively robust realm. He and his successors set about organizing a system of governance that drew from Visigothic traditions, local customs, and the emergent needs of a kingdom in its infancy.

Religion played a central role in forming and consolidating the Asturian Kingdom. Christianity was not just a faith but a unifying force and a source of legitimacy for the fledgling monarchy. Churches and monasteries were among the first institutions to be established, serving multiple roles - as places of worship, centers of learning, and repositories of culture and knowledge. The construction of these religious structures, often in the distinctive pre-Romanesque style, symbolized the kingdom's commitment to preserving and nurturing its Christian identity. It was perceived as a bastion of Christianity, a defiant stand against the spread of Islam in the peninsula. The Asturian monarchy adopted the mantle of the defenders of the Christian faith, an image that would be cultivated and revered throughout the Reconquista.

A crucial aspect of state-building was the codification of laws. Drawing upon the legal traditions of the Visigoths, Roman law, and local customs, the Asturian rulers began codifying laws to provide a legal framework for governance, justice, and social order. These laws addressed various aspects of daily life, from property

rights and trade regulations to criminal justice and civil disputes, laying the groundwork for a structured society.

Militarily, the kingdom was in a constant state of vigilance
and expansion. The Asturian monarchs recognized the importance of a strong military to defend their existing territories and push back against the Umayyad forces. Fortifications
were built, and a network of lookout posts was established
throughout the kingdom. Military campaigns were periodically launched to reclaim territories, pushing the kingdom's
boundaries southward inching closer to the ultimate goal of
reconquering Hispania.

Economic sustainability was crucial for the kingdom's via-
bility. Efforts were made to foster trade and agriculture, the
twin pillars of the Asturian economy. Trade routes were established and protected, facilitating the exchange of goods both
within the kingdom and with neighboring regions. Agriculture
was given special attention, introducing new crops and farming
techniques, boosting productivity, and ensuring food security
for the kingdom's inhabitants.

The social and cultural fabric of the Asturian Kingdom was
woven from diverse threads. While Christian traditions and
Visigothic heritage were predominant, there was also an ac-
knowledgment of the region's pre-Christian past and the various cultural influences that had shaped it over the centuries.
The Asturian monarchy encouraged the preservation of old
customs and the development of new cultural expressions, fostering a sense of Asturian identity.

The early years of the Asturian Kingdom were a period of foundational significance. From establishing governance and legal systems to fortifying defenses and nurturing the economy, the efforts of the early Asturian rulers set the stage for a kingdom that would endure the trials of time. These foundational years highlight the resilience, foresight, and determination of a people and their leaders in carving out a realm that would become the beacon of the Christian Reconquista.

DYNAMICS OF COEXISTENCE

The early-medieval Iberian Peninsula was a crucible of cultures, where the destinies of Christianity, Islam, and Judaism intertwined in a complex dance of coexistence, conflict, and collaboration. This era was not just a time of religious and political struggle, but also a period of cultural and intellectual exchange that would leave an indelible mark on the history of Europe and the Mediterranean.

With the Umayyad conquest altering the religious landscape of the Iberian Peninsula, the northern regions, especially Asturias, emerged as the heartland of Christian resistance. Christianity survived and thrived in these rugged lands, adapting to the new realities and challenges. The Asturian Kingdom became a symbol of Christian defiance, a beacon for those who yearned for the return of a Christian Iberia.

Churches and monasteries played a pivotal role. They were more than just places of worship; they were the custodians of Christian culture and heritage. In the seclusion of these religious sanctuaries, monks and clerics worked diligently to preserve the religious texts, chronicles, and knowledge of the pre-Islamic era.

Monasteries like San Juan de la Peña, Santo Toribio de Liébana, and San Millán de la Cogolla became centers of learning, spirituality, and resistance.

The Christian faith in the Asturian Kingdom and other northern territories took on a heightened spiritual symbolism. It was a link to a past that predated Islamic rule, a connection to the Visigothic heritage, and a marker of cultural identity. In these regions, Christianity was infused with a sense of mission and destiny. The narrative of the Reconquista, as a holy crusade to reclaim lost lands, was deeply rooted in this renewed Christian fervor.

Alongside preserving religious and cultural traditions, there was a blossoming of Christian art and architecture. The pre-Romanesque style, unique to the region, flourished in these years, with churches and monasteries adorned with intricate carvings, frescoes, and religious iconography. This artistic expression was an aesthetic endeavor and a statement of cultural and religious identity.

The clergy in these Christian territories played a significant role. They were spiritual leaders, advocates, and sometimes participants in military campaigns against the Umayyads. The church lent moral and sometimes material support to the Christian cause, reinforcing the notion of the Reconquista as a divinely ordained mission.

The establishment of pilgrimage routes, most notably the Camino de Santiago, contributed to the religious and cultural cohesion of Christian Iberia. These routes attracted pilgrims from across Europe, fostering a sense of shared faith and purpose. They were pathways of religious devotion, cultural exchange, and even political networking, strengthening the Christian resolve across the peninsula.

Christianity in the early medieval Iberian Peninsula, especially in the northern regions under the shadow of Umayyad rule, was marked by resilience and resistance. It evolved to become a religion, a symbol of cultural identity, and a rallying point for the Reconquista.

The churches, monasteries, clergy, and faithful played a crucial role in keeping the Christian legacy alive, setting the stage for the centuries-long struggle to reclaim the peninsula.

***

Islam, arriving as both a religion and a political force, introduced a new paradigm in Hispania's governance, culture, and intellectual life. The Umayyad caliphs, setting up their capital in Córdoba, laid the foundations for an Islamic society to become renowned for its sophistication, tolerance, and cultural achievements.

Under the Umayyads, Al-Andalus witnessed an unprecedented flourishing of arts and culture. With its iconic horseshoe arches, ornate calligraphy, and intricate tilework, Islamic architecture gave rise to stunning edifices like the Great Mosque of Córdoba. This architectural splendor was matched by advancements in the arts - from the delicate craftsmanship of artisans to the evocative poetry and music that echoed in the courtyards of Al-Andalus.

Perhaps one of the most enduring legacies of Islamic rule in Hispania was the intellectual awakening it fostered. Córdoba and other cities in Al-Andalus became learning centers, attracting scholars, scientists, and philosophers from across the Muslim world and Europe.

The translation movement, wherein significant works of ancient Greek, Persian, and Roman scholars were translated into Arabic, played a crucial role in preserving and enriching the global body of knowledge. Advances in fields such as astronomy, medicine, mathematics, and philosophy significantly contributed to the intellectual heritage of the medieval world.

The Umayyad caliphs established an administrative and legal framework in Al-Andalus that was innovative and pragmatic. Islamic law (Sharia) was the foundation, but the Umayyads also incorporated elements from the existing Visigothic systems and the customs of the diverse populace they governed. This governance approach helped maintain social order and justice in a multicultural society.

The Islamic rule brought with it a surge in economic activity and prosperity. Al-Andalus became a hub of international trade, connecting the Muslim world with the Christian kingdoms of Europe. Agricultural innovations, such as introducing new crops and irrigation techniques, transformed the landscape and boosted the economy. Markets in Al-Andalus buzzed with goods from as far as India and Sub-Saharan Africa, making it one of the most prosperous regions in medieval Europe.

Islam on the Iberian Peninsula under the Umayyads ushered in a new horizon of religious, cultural, and intellectual enlightenment. Al-Andalus, under Islamic rule, emerged as a beacon of learning, tolerance, and prosperity, leaving a legacy that transcended its borders and time.

The Jewish communities experienced a period of relative tolerance and prosperity, a stark contrast to the often oppressive conditions under the Visigothic Christian rule that preceded the Islamic conquest. The dhimmi status granted them certain protections and allowed them to practice their religion in exchange for a tax. This relative autonomy enabled Jewish communities to thrive culturally and economically.

Jews played a pivotal role in the intellectual and cultural life of Al-Andalus. They contributed to medicine, science, philosophy, and poetry and were instrumental in translating classical texts. Jewish scholars like Maimonides and Judah Halevi made significant contributions that resonated beyond the borders of Al-Andalus.

Economically, Jews were vital to the prosperity of Al-Andalus. As merchants and traders, they leveraged their extensive networks that spanned the Christian and Islamic worlds. Their role as intermediaries facilitated both trade and cultural and intellectual exchanges between the Muslim and Christian territories.

In the Christian territories of the north, the situation of the Jewish communities was more complex and varied. During periods of enlightened rule, Jews found opportunities to prosper and contribute to the economic and cultural spheres. However, these periods were often interspersed with intolerance and persecution, especially during political upheaval or religious fervor.

The Jewish experience in early-medieval Iberia, straddling the realms of Christian and Islamic rulers, is a testament to the enduring spirit of a community that continually adapted to changing circumstances.

The coexistence of these three faiths in the early medieval period was a time of profound interplay among Christianity, Islam, and Judaism. This era, characterized by both coexistence and conflict, shaped the peninsula's religious, cultural, and intellectual contours.

FUSION OF KNOWLEDGE

Under Islamic rule in Al-Andalus, the Iberian Peninsula became a crucible for scientific advancement. The translation movement, spearheaded in cities like Córdoba and Toledo, saw scholars translating works of ancient Greek, Roman, and Persian science and philosophy into Arabic. These translations, which later made their way into Christian Europe, were instrumental in preserving and expanding the knowledge inherited from the ancient world.

In medicine, Jewish and Muslim physicians, such as Maimonides and Averroes, made significant contributions, drawing upon both ancient and contemporary knowledge.

In astronomy, the observatories of Al-Andalus became centers for studying the stars, influencing navigational techniques across the known world. Mathematics saw a renaissance with the introduction of Arabic numerals and the concept of zero, a paradigm shift that revolutionized European mathematics.

A remarkable interchange of styles and techniques marked the artistic realm of medieval Iberia. Islamic art, emphasizing intricate geometric patterns and calligraphy, influenced the architectural and decorative arts throughout the peninsula. The Mozarabic and Romanesque styles reflected Islamic influences in Christian territories, especially in ornamental motifs and architectural designs.

Literature and poetry flourished. In Al-Andalus, poetry became a celebrated art form practiced by Muslims, Christians, and Jews. The works of poets like Ibn Hazm and Al-Mu'tamid are examples of the rich literary heritage of this period. The epic tales and ballads of the Christian kingdoms, often recounting battles and heroes of the Reconquista, added to the diverse literary landscape.

The cultural and scientific achievements of Iberia did not remain confined to the peninsula. This knowledge spread to the rest of Europe through trade, conquest, and scholarly exchange. The schools and libraries of Al-Andalus, particularly in Toledo, became centers for the transmission of this knowledge to European scholars, laying the groundwork for the Renaissance.

Religious and cultural institutions played a crucial role in fostering this exchange. Churches, mosques, synagogues, and madrasas were not only places of worship but also centers of learning and artistic expression. These institutions often provided patronage to scholars, artists, and poets, enabling the flowering of culture and science.

***

The architectural legacy of medieval Iberia further exemplifies the profound level of cultural exchange. The interlacing of Islamic, Christian, and Jewish architectural elements created unique styles that symbolized the era's composite culture. The use of horseshoe arches, intricate mosaics, and ornamental calligraphy in churches and palaces, alongside the traditional Romanesque and Gothic styles, showcased an aesthetic fusion unparalleled in medieval Europe. The Alhambra in Granada, with its stunning Islamic architecture, and the Cathedral of Santiago de Compostela, a Romanesque art masterpiece, epitomize the period's architectural splendor.

In philosophy and thought, medieval Iberia was a ground for interfaith dialogue and intellectual exchange. Islamic, Christian, and Jewish philosophers engaged with each other's works, leading to a cross-pollination of ideas. The works of Averroes (Ibn Rushd), a Muslim philosopher, were profoundly influential in the Christian tradition. Similarly, Jewish thinkers like Maimonides, who were versed in Islamic and Jewish traditions, played a pivotal role in bridging different philosophical worlds.

The music of Iberia during this period was also indicative of the cultural synthesis. The exchange of musical instruments, such as the lute (oud), and the blending of musical styles led to the development of unique genres that would influence the musical landscape of Europe and the Mediterranean.

The vibrant economic and trade networks of medieval Iberia facilitated the exchange of goods, ideas, and culture. Cities like Córdoba, Seville, and Toledo became bustling centers of commerce where merchants and artisans of different faiths interacted, sharing techniques and styles. These interactions fostered an environment where innovation and creativity flourished.

While the era was marked by periods of relative tolerance, it is essential to acknowledge its complexities and the limits of this coexistence. Times of conflict and intolerance punctuated the history of medieval Iberia, reminding us that the interplay of cultures was often a delicate balance. Yet, the overarching legacy of the period is one of mutual enrichment.

This era of convergence, with its artistic, scientific, and philosophical achievements, stands as a beacon of the collaborative potential of human societies.

THE POLITICAL PARADIGM

The Umayyad conquest of the Iberian Peninsula marked a seismic shift in the region's political landscape. The arrival of Islamic rule transformed the governance structures and redefined the power dynamics in Hispania. The Umayyads, ruling from Córdoba, established a centralized administration that was advanced for its time, bringing a level of sophistication and efficiency previously unseen in the region. This new political order not only unified the diverse territories of the peninsula under one rule but also introduced new concepts of law, taxation, and public administration.

The Umayyads displayed remarkable diplomatic skill in governing this diverse population. They struck a balance between asserting Islamic dominance and accommodating the religious and cultural practices of Christians and Jews. This approach was not just pragmatic but also a reflection of the Islamic teachings on tolerance and the historical practice of Muslim governance. The use of agreements, or treaties, with Christian communities and the recognition of the legal autonomy of Jewish communities were examples of this diplomatic approach.

The administrative system established by the Umayyads in Al-Andalus was advanced for its time. It was characterized by a high degree of organization, with a clear hierarchy and defined roles within the government. The Umayyads implemented systems of taxation and public administration that were effective yet sensitive to the social dynamics of the region. This system ensured the state's efficient running and revenue collection while minimizing social discontent.

The Umayyads allowed for a significant degree of cultural plurality. This was evident in the arts, sciences, and commerce, which saw contributions from all communities. This confluence of ideas influenced Islamic culture in Al-Andalus, particularly in architecture, poetry, and philosophy, leading to a unique Andalusian flavor that distinguished it from other parts of the Muslim world.

While this was a source of strength, it also challenged social harmony. Issues of religious and cultural identity occasionally led to tensions. The Umayyads had to constantly navigate these complexities, balancing maintaining Islamic authority and ensuring the welfare of all communities. Civil unrest and rebellion were not uncommon, requiring military response and diplomatic negotiation.

These instances were symptomatic of the underlying challenges in maintaining harmony in a society fragmented by differing beliefs, interests, and loyalties. Religious differences, particularly among extremist factions, occasionally led to conflict. Economic grievances, such as unfair taxation or resource allocation, also sparked discontent, especially among the rural and urban poor. Power struggles within the Umayyad dynasty or between rival aristocratic families sometimes spilled over into wider societal conflicts.

One significant example of rebellion in Al-Andalus was the Berber Revolt in the early 8th century. The Berbers, originally from North Africa and instrumental in the Umayyad conquest of Hispania, felt marginalized and exploited under the new regime. Their revolt was a significant challenge to Umayyad authority, necessitating a robust military response combined with efforts to address their grievances.

The Umayyad rulers often had to use military force to quell rebellions and restore order. Their approach varied from direct military intervention to strategic fortification of critical areas. While effective in suppressing immediate threats, military campaigns were often only part of the solution, as they addressed the symptoms rather than the underlying causes of unrest.

Recognizing that military action alone was insufficient to ensure long-term stability, the Umayyads employed diplomacy and negotiation. They engaged with community leaders, negotiated settlements, and sometimes made concessions to address the root causes of discontent. This approach was particularly effective when grievances were economic or administrative rather than ideological.

To preempt unrest, the Umayyads implemented strategies to integrate various communities into the fabric of Al-Andalus. This included equitable representation in administrative roles, fair taxation policies, and initiatives to promote cultural and religious tolerance—these efforts aimed to foster a sense of belonging and loyalty among the diverse populace.

Each instance of unrest or rebellion in Al-Andalus served as a learning experience for the Umayyad rulers. These events highlighted the complexities of governing a diverse society and the need for a balanced approach that combined firm governance with sensitivity to the needs and aspirations of different communities.

The civil unrest and rebellion under the Umayyads reflected the challenges inherent in managing a pluralistic society. The Umayyad response to these challenges, a blend of military might, diplomatic negotiation, and efforts at social integration, underscores the delicate balance required in governing a diverse and multifaceted populace.

NEW CHRISTIAN KINGDOMS

The success of Asturias inspired the formation of other Christian kingdoms in the north, each playing a crucial role in the Reconquista narrative. The Kingdom of León, Castile, Navarre, and Aragon emerged as significant power centers, gradually expanding their territories at the expense of the Muslim-ruled regions.

Though often engaged in internal rivalries, these kingdoms shared the common goal of reclaiming Iberian lands for Christendom.

Following the establishment of the Asturian Kingdom, the Kingdom of León emerged as a formidable force in the Reconquista. Initially part of the Asturian realm, León gained prominence under the leadership of ambitious monarchs who expanded its territories southward.

The city of León, with its strategic location, became a vital center of political and military power. The Kingdom of León was instrumental in pushing the frontiers of Christendom further into the heart of the peninsula, laying the groundwork for future expansions.

Castile, originally a county within the Kingdom of León, became a crucial player in the Reconquista. Its transformation into an independent kingdom marked a significant shift in northern Iberia's power balance. Castilian leaders, such as Fernán González and later El Cid, became legendary figures in the Reconquista narrative. Castile's military prowess and strategic marriages expanded its influence, eventually leading to the union with León and the formation of a powerful Christian bloc.

The Kingdom of Navarre, situated in the Pyrenees, played a unique role in the socio-political landscape of the Reconquista. Navarre was a nexus of Christian and Muslim interactions as a border kingdom. Its monarchs navigated a complex diplomatic path, aligning with Muslim rulers and joining forces with fellow Christian kingdoms. Navarre's strategic position made it a key player in controlling important trade routes and mountain passes.

Aragon's rise from a county within the Carolingian Empire to a significant kingdom in the Reconquista was marked by strategic expansion and political acumen. The union of Aragon with the County of Barcelona under the Crown of Aragon created a formidable force in northeastern Iberia. Aragonese monarchs, such as Alfonso I and James I, led successful campaigns into Muslim-held territories, extending their influence into Valencia and the Balearic Islands.

The relationships among the Christian kingdoms of León, Castile, Navarre, and Aragon were characterized by a complex interplay of alliances, marriages, and rivalries. While united by the common objective of the Reconquista, these kingdoms also pursued territorial and political ambitions, leading to conflicts and power struggles. The dynastic unions and treaties among these kingdoms were instrumental in consolidating Christian power in the peninsula.

The expansion of these Christian kingdoms reshaped the socio-political fabric of the Iberian Peninsula. The Reconquista was a military endeavor and a process of territorial integration, cultural assimilation, and socio-political restructuring. The newly conquered territories underwent significant changes as they were integrated into the Christian kingdoms, with shifts in land ownership, population movements, and the imposition of new legal and administrative systems. Each kingdom, with its unique characteristics and ambitions, contributed to the gradual reclamation of the Iberian Peninsula from Muslim rule.

KINGDOM OF LEÓN

Nestled in the rugged landscapes of northern Iberia, the Kingdom of León rose like a phoenix from the ashes of the Asturian Kingdom. Initially an integral limb of the Asturian body, León soon unfurled its wings, soaring under the guidance of visionary monarchs who saw in its destiny a role far beyond the confines of Asturias. The transfer of the capital to León was a declaration of intent, a clarion call signaling the kingdom's rising ambitions and burgeoning influence.

León's heart, the city itself, stood at the crossroads of history and geography. A city that lay at the vital juncture of trade routes, it was more than a mere settlement—it was the drumbeat of Reconquista, pulsating with political intrigue, economic vigor, and military strategy. Its strategic position was a spear in the side of Muslim-held territories, a launching pad for expeditions that would etch the kingdom's name in history

Under the banners of León, monarchs such as Ordoño I and Ramiro II embarked on audacious campaigns that would see the kingdom's boundaries stretch ever southward. Their conquests were not mere territorial grabs but calculated moves designed to fortify Christian dominions and carve out a buffer against the Islamic tide.

The roles played by its monarchs were pivotal in shaping its destiny. Leaders like Ordoño I and Ramiro II were not just rulers; they were architects of an expanding Christian frontier. Under their reign, León's banners marched southward, extending the kingdom's influence and presence into territories long held by Muslim powers.

Ordoño I's reign marked a significant period of expansion for León. His military campaigns were driven by a strategic vision to secure and strengthen the kingdom's southern borders. Recognizing the importance of establishing a stronghold in the Douro River valley, Ordoño led successful expeditions that pushed León's frontiers beyond the Cantabrian Mountains. His conquests in the northwest, including victories against the Moors, solidified León's position as a rising power in the Reconquista.

Ramiro II, inheriting a kingdom on the ascent, continued the expansionist policies of his predecessors with zeal and determination. Known for his military prowess, Ramiro II led daring raids into Muslim territories, demonstrating his tactical prowess and commitment to the Christian cause. Whether historical or legendary, his victory at the Battle of Alhandic (or Clavijo) became a symbol of Leonese valor and divine favor in the struggle against Islamic rule.

The conquests of these monarchs were far more than mere expansions of territory; they were integral steps in securing the future of the Christian kingdoms in Iberia. Each campaign, each battle won, served to fortify León's position both politically and militarily. The territories brought under León's control provided vital resources and strategic depth, essential in the continuing struggle against the Muslim states to the south.

As León's borders expanded, so too did its socio-political complexities. Integrating new territories into the Leonese domain was a task that demanded astute governance. With a blend of military might and administrative acumen, the Leonese kings wove these new lands into the kingdom's feudal fabric. Churches rose, monasteries dotted the landscape, and new settlements burgeoned under the kingdom's protective gaze, all contributing to the entrenchment of Christian authority.

Beyond its military and political endeavors, León emerged as a bastion of culture and religious life. Its monasteries became beacons of learning and spiritual contemplation, while its scriptoria hummed with the work of scribes preserving the wisdom of ages. The architectural grandeur of the Basilica of San Isidoro was not just a testament to Leonese artistry but a symbol of the kingdom's role as a custodian of the Christian faith.

In the intricate ballet of Iberian politics, León danced with both grace and guile. Its monarchs, adept at diplomacy, forged alliances with Christian neighbors and negotiated pacts with Muslim emirs.

These alliances, often sealed with marriages or treaties, were pivotal in cementing León's status and coordinating efforts against mutual foes.

The Kingdom of León played a pivotal role in shaping medieval Iberia. Its journey from an Asturian offshoot to a powerhouse of the Christian reconquest exemplifies its ambition, resilience, and strategic brilliance.

CASTILE'S ASCENDANCY

In the rugged landscape of northern Iberia, the story of Castile's rise from a modest county to a sovereign kingdom captures the essence of ambition and resilience. Initially serving as the shield against Muslim incursions at the frontier of the Kingdom of León, Castile carved its own path, its identity forged in the crucible of conflict and opportunity. Its leaders, seizing the moment as the power in León wavered, steered Castile toward independence and prominence.

Fernán González, a name etched in the annals of Castilian history, was the architect of this transformation. As the first autonomous Count of Castile, his vision transcended mere defense of his lands. He waged campaigns not only to ward off external threats but also to forge a unified Castilian identity. His victories against Muslim forces and strategic governance solidified Castile's standing as pivotal in the Reconquista narrative.

González understood that for Castile to emerge as a strong and independent entity, it needed a cohesive identity to unify its diverse population under a common banner. His military campaigns were a blend of tactical brilliance and strategic foresight. He led his forces against Muslim armies, pushing back the frontiers and reclaiming lands that had been lost.

These victories were not just about territorial expansion; they were statements of Castile's growing power and its role in the larger context of the Reconquista. Under his command, Castile transformed from a reactive borderland to an assertive kingdom, actively shaping Iberian history.

One of Fernán González's most significant contributions was fostering a unified Castilian identity among his people. He nurtured a sense of shared destiny and pride among the Castilians, crucial in a landscape fragmented by various loyalties and regional identities. This sense of identity was vital in rallying the people of Castile for the Reconquista's challenges and establishing a legacy that would endure through the centuries.

González's role as a ruler was marked by strategic governance. He implemented administrative reforms and policies that strengthened the internal structure of Castile. These reforms ensured better management of resources, improved defense capabilities, and enhanced the welfare of his subjects. His governance style laid the groundwork for the future administrative systems of Castile as a kingdom.

The legacy of Fernán González is not just as a military leader but as a founding father of Castilian independence. His life and achievements became ingrained in Castilian lore, inspiring future generations to continue the struggle for autonomy and identity in the face of external threats.

Rodrigo Díaz de Vivar, known to history and legend as El Cid, stands as the quintessential hero of Castile, a figure whose life and deeds have become an integral part of the Reconquista's narrative. His story, woven into the fabric of Castilian identity, represents more than just military triumphs; it symbolizes bravery, honor, and unwavering dedication to one's cause.

El Cid's military career was remarkable for its breadth and impact. Not confined to serving just one master or kingdom, his sword was sworn to various rulers, both Christian and Muslim. This unique aspect of his life illustrates the complex interplay of loyalties and alliances in medieval Spain. His ability to navigate this intricate landscape without losing sight of his ultimate loyalty to Castile and Christendom is a testament to his diplomatic guile and personal charisma.

The capture of Valencia was one of El Cid's most significant military achievements. Laying siege to the city, which was a jewel in the crown of Al-Andalus, El Cid demonstrated his martial prowess, strategic foresight, and leadership qualities.

El Cid's legacy extends beyond his battlefield victories. He emerged as a unifier, a figure who symbolized the potential for cohesion and collective purpose among the Christian kingdoms of Iberia in a time of fragmentation and rivalry. His life and deeds inspired a sense of shared identity and destiny, crucial in the sustained effort of the Reconquista.

His life, embellished over time into legend, became the subject of epic poems and ballads. The "Cantar de Mio Cid," a seminal work of Spanish literature, immortalized his exploits, portraying him as the ideal knight, loyal to his king, fearless in battle, and just to his followers. These stories passed down through generations, have cemented El Cid's status as a cultural and national icon.

El Cid's influence extends far beyond the historical and into the realms of cultural and national identity. In him, the ideals of the Reconquista - bravery, honor, and the struggle for a righteous cause - found their most potent expression.

El Cid occupies a place of honor in Castile's history and the Reconquista's broader narrative. His extraordinary life, blending historical fact with legendary lore, continues to inspire and captivate. As a warrior, a leader, and a unifying figure, his legacy endures as a symbol of the enduring spirit and aspirations of Castile and the Reconquista.

The military strategy of Castile, a blend of audacious offensives and astute fortifications, drove its expansion. Its leaders knew they needed to fortify their conquests to sustain their gains against the Muslim south. Thus, Castilian expansion was marked by establishing strongholds that secured newly conquered lands and served as bases for further incursions.

Castile also played a masterful game of alliances and marriages. Strategic matrimonial ties with other Christian kingdoms bolstered its position, while alliances, sometimes even with Muslim rulers, were vital to navigating the complex political landscape.

These alliances were crucial for securing Castile's borders and legitimizing its expansion.

The union of Castile with León under King Ferdinand I marked a turning point in the Reconquista. This blending of two dominant Christian kingdoms dramatically altered the balance of power, creating a formidable force in northern Iberia. This union was not just a convergence of territories but a fusion of ambitions and resources, accelerating the pace of the Christian reconquest.

Castile's transformation from a frontier buffer to a vanguard of the Reconquista is a narrative of strategic ingenuity, military might, and unwavering resolve. Its role in the reclamation of the Iberian Peninsula was instrumental in shaping the course of medieval history. Castile's story, rich in battles won and alliances forged is a testament to the indomitable spirit of a kingdom that played a central role in the socio-political renaissance of medieval Iberia.

NAVARRE IN THE RECONQUISTA

Perched in the shadow of the Pyrenees, the Kingdom of Navarre occupied a pivotal position in the drama of the Reconquista. Its geographical location, straddling the boundary between the Christian north and the Muslim south, endowed it with a unique role. With its rugged landscapes and strategic passes, Navarre was not just a kingdom but a bridge between divergent worlds.

The rulers of Navarre, acutely aware of their kingdom's strategic significance, mastered the art of diplomacy in an era marked by shifting alliances and perennial conflicts. They maneuvered through the complex socio-political landscape of the time, sometimes forming alliances with Muslim emirates to counterbalance the power of neighboring Christian kingdoms and, at other times, joining forces with their Christian counterparts in a united front against Muslim advances. This nuanced diplomacy was crucial in maintaining Navarre's sovereignty and influence.

Navarre's unique position as a border kingdom meant its rulers had to balance power dynamics and religious affiliations constantly. They were guardians of the Christian frontier, yet they recognized the benefits of peaceful coexistence and trade with Muslim states. This delicate balancing act was a hallmark of Navarrese politics, reflecting a pragmatic approach to the challenges of the time.

The Kingdom of Navarre's control over crucial mountain passes and trade routes was a significant aspect of its power. These routes were lifelines for commerce, connecting the Iberian Peninsula with the rest of Europe. Navarrese monarchs capitalized on this, levying taxes and tolls and thus accruing wealth and resources vital for the kingdom's economic stability and military endeavors.

Navarre's approach to the Reconquista was distinguished by its duality. On one hand, as a Christian kingdom, it was inherently aligned with the overarching goal of reclaiming Iberian lands from Muslim rule. Navarrese rulers, like their counterparts in other Christian territories, often engaged in military campaigns aimed at pushing back the Islamic frontiers. However, Navarre often adopted a pragmatic approach to its Muslim neighbors, unlike some of the more zealous kingdoms.

Navarrese monarchs were known for their adept diplomatic maneuvering, often forming alliances with Muslim rulers when it suited their strategic interests. These alliances, sometimes considered controversial by their Christian allies, were part of a broader strategy to maintain Navarre's independence and influence. Navarre could leverage its position to exert influence over the Reconquista's progress by aligning with Muslim emirates, sometimes slowing it down or redirecting its focus.

While diplomacy played a key role, Navarre also engaged in direct military action as part of the Reconquista. The kingdom's troops participated in skirmishes and battles along the border-lands, contributing to the shifting boundaries between Christian and Muslim rule. Though often localized, these military engage-ments had broader implications for the overall power dynamics of the peninsula.

With its nuanced stance, Navarre often acted as a mediator in conflicts between Christian and Muslim states. Its ability to main-tain relationships across religious and political divides allowed it to influence negotiations and treaties, which had significant im-plications. Navarre's multifaceted role in the Reconquista also had cultural and religious implications. The kingdom became a cross-roads where ideas, traditions, and beliefs from both Christian and Muslim worlds intersected. This intermingling enriched Navarre's heritage and contributed to the medieval Iberian culture.

Navarre's role in the Reconquista was symbolic of the complex-ity and diversity of the period. Its ability to navigate the shift-ing sands of Iberian politics, balancing military engagements with strategic diplomacy, positioned it as a critical player in the struggle between Christian and Muslim powers. The legacy of Navarre in the Reconquista is that of a kingdom that deftly managed the challenges of its unique position, influencing the course of history in medieval Iberia.

CROWN OF ARAGON

The ascent of Aragon from a humble county to a dominant kingdom in northeastern Iberia is a tale of political savvy, strategic marriages, and military prowess. Its transformation into a formidable force played a crucial role in shaping the history of medieval Spain.

In the early chapters of the Reconquista, Aragon was but a small player, a county under the vast umbrella of the Carolingian Empire. Yet, within its veins pulsed the ambition to rise above its station. The turning point came with the union of Aragon and the County of Barcelona, a marriage not just of lands but of destinies. This union birthed the Crown of Aragon, a political entity that would leave an indelible mark on the Iberian Peninsula.

Aragon's expansion during the Reconquista was not just a series of battles and conquests. Under the guidance of shrewd monarchs, Aragon extended its influence through military might and, alliances and marriages that intertwined its fate with other peninsula powers. This expansion was a dance of diplomacy and warfare, as Aragon slowly but steadily carved out its territory in the contested lands of Iberia.

Aragon's rise is illuminated by the figures of Alfonso I and James I, monarchs whose reigns were pivotal in the kingdom's history. Alfonso I, nicknamed 'the Battler,' was a king whose military campaigns defined his reign. His aggressive forays into Muslim-held territories were not mere skirmishes but well-planned operations aimed at expanding Aragon's dominion.

His conquests, particularly in the Ebro Valley, significantly altered the political map of northern Iberia. Under his rule, Aragon pushed its frontiers southward, gaining territory and disrupting the balance of power in the region. Alfonso's campaigns were more than territorial expansions; they were statements of Aragon's growing strength and its role in the Christian reconquest of the peninsula.

James I, known as "the Conqueror," inherited a kingdom already on the rise and propelled it to greater heights. His reign was marked by successful campaigns that further expanded Aragon's territory. The conquest of Valencia was a crowning achievement, showcasing not only his military prowess but also his strategic prowess. This victory was crucial in providing Aragon with a valuable foothold in the eastern part of the peninsula, opening new economic and political opportunities.

The conquest of the Balearic Islands was another significant milestone under James I. It extended Aragon's influence into the Mediterranean, transforming the kingdom into a naval power.

This expansion was not just a demonstration of military might but a strategic move that enhanced Aragon's role in Mediterranean trade and politics, boosting its economic and cultural growth.

The legacies of Alfonso I and James I are intertwined with the very identity of Aragon during the Reconquista. They were leaders who understood the importance of both military might and strategic diplomacy. Their reigns saw the transformation of Aragon from a regional power to a significant player on the broader stage of Iberian politics.

Their conquests brought diverse peoples and lands under the Aragonese crown, necessitating administrative and cultural integration. This period of expansion under their rule also blended various cultural influences, enriching the kingdom's cultural and social fabric.

Alfonso I and James I were more than just monarchs; they were visionaries who significantly influenced Aragon's history. Their military campaigns and strategic decisions laid the foundation for a kingdom that played a pivotal role in the Reconquista and the shaping of medieval Spain.

As Aragon expanded, it brought a diverse range of territories and peoples under its fold. This expansion necessitated a transformation in its socio-political structures. The integration of new lands and cultures, establishing legal and administrative systems, and promoting settlement and development in these regions were essential aspects of Aragon's rule.

Aragon stands out as a kingdom that skillfully navigated the tides of change and conflict. From its humble beginnings to its rise as a major power in northeastern Iberia and the Mediterranean, Aragon's story is one of strategic expansion, political cleverness, and cultural integration.

Its role in the Reconquista was not just as a military power but as a kingdom that shaped medieval Spain's political, cultural, and economic landscape.

Alliances and Power Dynamics

In the labyrinthine world of medieval Iberia, the Reconquista was as much won by diplomacy as by the sword. The era was marked by a dynamic interplay of alliances and power shifts, where kingdoms and emirates, both Christian and Muslim, continuously recalibrated their relationships in response to the ever-changing political landscape.

The Reconquista, often perceived solely as a prolonged military conflict, was equally a stage for intricate diplomatic maneuvering. Christian kingdoms and Muslim emirates recognized the power of alliances – sometimes forged, sometimes broken – as tools to further their interests and consolidate their power. These alliances were not static; they were as fluid as the shifting sands, often driven by pragmatic considerations rather than religious or ideological affinities.

Among the Christian kingdoms of León, Castile, Navarre, and Aragon, alliances were frequently formed and dissolved, driven by the dual desires of cooperation against a common Muslim adversary and competition for territorial and political dominance.

Marriages between royal families, treaties of mutual assistance, and non-aggression pacts were common, yet so were conflicts over borders and successions. These internal Christian dynamics significantly influenced the course and nature of the Reconquista. This delicate balance of cooperation and competition was a defining feature of the period, shaping the strategies and outcomes.

While sharing a common religious identity and a unified goal of reclaiming Iberian lands from Muslim control, these Christian kingdoms were also driven by their aspirations for territorial expansion and political influence. Alliances, often cemented by marriages between royal families, were strategic moves aimed at strengthening positions against Muslim powers and neighboring Christian rivals. These marriages were not just personal unions but were also pivotal political events that could shift the balance of power in the region.

Treaties of mutual assistance and pacts of non-aggression were common among these kingdoms. They were essential tools of diplomacy, used to secure borders, gain time for internal consolidation, or prepare for larger military campaigns. However, the fluid political landscape of the Reconquista meant that such agreements were often temporary, subject to the changing priorities and ambitions of the kingdoms involved.

Despite these alliances, conflicts among the Christian kingdoms were frequent. Disputes over borders were common, as each kingdom sought to expand its territory at the expense of its neighbors. Succession crises, a common occurrence in medieval monarchies, often provided opportunities for neighboring kingdoms to intervene in each other's affairs, either to support a favored claimant or to expand their influence.

The alternating cycles of alliance and rivalry among the Christian kingdoms profoundly impacted the Reconquista. These dynamics sometimes facilitated united fronts against Muslim territories, leading to significant conquests and advances. At other times, they resulted in missed opportunities, as internal Christian conflicts diverted resources and focus away from the fight against Muslim powers.

A pragmatic assessment of power, opportunity, and risk guided the decisions and actions of these states. Their relationships, marked by cooperation and competition, significantly influenced the pace and nature of the Christian reconquest of the Iberian Peninsula. Understanding these internal dynamics is vital to comprehending the broader narrative marked by a constant balancing act between shared goals and individual ambitions.

On the Muslim side, the landscape was equally complex. The Umayyad Caliphate in Córdoba, and later the various Taifa kingdoms that emerged following its collapse, navigated a precarious path of survival and dominance. Alliances with Christian powers were common, often as a counterbalance against more immediate threats from neighboring Muslim rulers or other Christian kingdoms.

The politics within these Muslim states were characterized by a similar blend of competition and cooperation, reflecting the diverse and often fragmented nature of Islamic rule in Iberia.

At its zenith, the Umayyad Caliphate was a powerhouse of cultural, economic, and military strength. However, internal strife and external pressures eventually led to its fragmentation, giving rise to the Taifa kingdoms. These smaller, often competing states were each driven by their ambitions and the need to assert their sovereignty in a rapidly changing political landscape.

The Taifa kingdoms were diverse in their cultural and political makeup, each carving out its territory and identity within the Iberian Peninsula. Their rulers, often ambitious and capable leaders, sought to maintain and expand their influence amidst the constant threat of external conquest and internal revolt. The Taifas were characterized by their cultural richness, economic prosperity, and political vulnerability.

In this era of political fragmentation, alliances across religious lines became a key survival strategy for many Muslim rulers. Aligning with Christian powers provided them much-needed support against more pressing threats, whether from aggressive neighboring Taifas or other Christian kingdoms seeking to expand their territories. These alliances were often pragmatic, driven by the immediate needs of survival and advantage rather than religious solidarity.

The Muslim rulers of Iberia had to balance the delicate equation of power and diplomacy constantly. This involved managing relationships with Christian kingdoms and navigating the complex web of rivalries and alliances within the Muslim community. The Taifa kingdoms, while culturally and economically vibrant, were often embroiled in conflicts with each other, each seeking to assert its dominance in the region.

The Umayyad Caliphate and the Taifa kingdoms navigated a precarious political landscape, marked by internal fragmentation and external challenges. The shifting alliances had a profound impact on the region's stability.

They sometimes led to periods of relative peace, with powers focusing inward on consolidation and development. In other instances, they precipitated conflicts, drawing various states into complex webs of war and intrigue. The fluid nature of these alliances meant that the balance of power was continually in flux, creating an environment of unpredictability and constant change.

In the shadow of the larger Christian and Muslim states, smaller powers and borderlands played crucial roles in the Reconquista's power dynamics. Border territories often switched hands, serving as buffers or strategic points of contention. Smaller states and principalities, while lacking the might of the larger kingdoms, used their strategic positions and diplomatic skills to navigate the turbulent waters of Iberian politics.

This era in medieval Iberia was defined not just by the clash of swords but also by the subtleties of diplomacy and alliance-building. The constantly shifting alliances and power dynamics among

Christian and Muslim states added layers of complexity, impacting the region's stability and shaping its future.

LEGACY OF THE DAWN

The early events of the Reconquista not only shaped the contours of medieval Iberian politics but also left an indelible imprint on Spain's cultural and historical identity. These seminal events created an enduring legacy, tracing their influence through the centuries and recognizing their role in shaping the Spain we know today.

The Reconquista laid the groundwork for the emergence of modern Spain. The early battles, alliances, and political maneuverings set in motion events that eventually led to the unification of disparate kingdoms into a single nation. The consolidation of territories under Christian rule, driven by the early successes and struggles of the Reconquista, was instrumental in forging a unified Spanish identity.

The interactions between Christian, Muslim, and Jewish communities during these tumultuous times led to a rich intermingling of artistic, architectural, and intellectual traditions. This cultural fusion is evident in the unique architectural styles of Spain, the cross-pollination in literature and philosophy, and the evolution of distinct Spanish art and music. The early Reconquista period, with its blend of cultures and ideas, set the stage for a rich, diverse cultural heritage that was uniquely Spanish.

The Reconquista also played a crucial role in shaping Spain's political landscape and thought. The notions of sovereignty, territorial integrity, and national identity that emerged during this period were fundamental in developing the Spanish state. The evolving concepts of kingship, governance, and law during the early Reconquista influenced the political institutions and philosophies that would later define the Spanish monarchy and government.

The enduring impact of the Reconquista is also seen in the complex history of religious and cultural coexistence in Spain. The legacy of this era is riddled with triumph and tragedy, marked by periods of remarkable tolerance and episodes of profound conflict. The history of the Reconquista serves as a reminder of both the potential for cultural and religious harmony and the dangers of intolerance and division.

The Reconquista story has been revisited and reinterpreted through the ages, reflecting the evolving understanding of Spain's past. It is a subject of academic study and a part of the collective memory and national identity. This saga continues to influence the perceptions and discourse in modern Spain.

The legacy of the early events of the Reconquista is a mosaic of cultural, political, and historical influences that have shaped the fabric of Spain. From the consolidation of its territories and the forging of its national identity to the rich cultural synthesis and the complex interplay of religions, the echoes of these early events continue to resonate in the Spain of today.

The Reconquista, particularly its dawn, is not just a historical period but a foundational epoch that has defined and continues to influence the trajectory of Spanish history.

TIMELINE OF KEY EVENTS

This timeline provides a brief overview of significant milestones during the Reconquista, offering a quick reference to the pivotal events that shaped this epochal period in Iberian history.

711 The Umayyad Conquest of Hispania

- The Muslim Moors, led by Tariq ibn Ziyad, cross the Strait of Gibraltar, marking the beginning of Islamic rule in the Iberian Peninsula.

718 Battle of Covadonga

- Pelayo, a Visigothic noble, led a successful rebellion against the Moors in Asturias, regarded as the starting point of the Reconquista.

722 Establishment of the Kingdom of Asturias

- The foundation of the Christian Kingdom of Asturias by Pelayo after his victory at Covadonga.

756 Establishment of the Umayyad Emirate of Córdoba

- Abd al-Rahman I established the Umayyad Emirate in Córdoba, asserting independence from the Abbasid Caliphate.

910 Formation of the Kingdom of León

- The Kingdom of León was formed as a successor state to the Kingdom of Asturias.

929 Rise of the Umayyad Caliphate of Córdoba

- Abd al-Rahman III declared himself Caliph, transforming the Umayyad Emirate into a Caliphate.

1031 Collapse of the Umayyad Caliphate and Rise of Taifa Kingdoms

- The Umayyad Caliphate disintegrated into multiple Taifa kingdoms.

1085 Fall of Toledo to Alfonso VI of León and Castile

- The strategic city of Toledo is captured by Christian forces, marking a significant milestone in the Reconquista.

1096 - 1102 El Cid's Conquest of Valencia

- Rodrigo Díaz de Vivar, known as El Cid, captures Valencia, temporarily establishing an independent principality.

1139 Establishment of the Kingdom of Portugal

- Afonso I declared the independence of Portugal from the Kingdom of León.

1212 Battle of Las Navas de Tolosa

- A crucial victory for Christian forces, significantly weakening Muslim power in the Iberian Peninsula.

1236 Conquest of Córdoba by Ferdinand III of Castile

- The historic city of Córdoba is recaptured from the Moors.

1238 Conquest of Valencia by James I of Aragon

- The city of Valencia is taken by James I, further expanding Aragon's territory in eastern Iberia.

1248 Fall of Seville to Christian Forces

- Seville, one of the last major Muslim strongholds, is captured by Ferdinand III of Castile.

1492 Fall of Granada and Completion of the Reconquista

- The Emirate of Granada, the last Muslim state in Iberia, surrendered to Ferdinand II of Aragon and Isabella I of Castile, marking the end of the Reconquista.

BIBLIOGRAPHY AND SOURCES

I n writing this book, these sources were indispensable. They served as foundational pillars, offering a wealth of historical data and cultural context to guide the narrative and ensure its authenticity. Each source was selected for its relevance and contribution to the understanding of the Reconquista.

These works are invaluable for readers wishing to delve further into the history of medieval Spain. They offer a comprehensive view of the period, covering everything from political machinations and military campaigns to cultural exchanges and architectural innovations.

Whether you are a casual enthusiast or a serious scholar, these sources open doors to a deeper appreciation and understanding of the Reconquista's legacy.

Primary Sources

1. Chronica Adefonsi Imperatoris - A chronicle detailing the reign of Alfonso VII of León and Castile.

2. Historia Roderici - A biography of Rodrigo Díaz de Vivar, known as El Cid.

3. Poema de Mio Cid - An epic poem that captures the legend of El Cid.

4. Cantar de las huestes de Igor - An Old East Slavic epic poem recounting the campaigns of Prince Igor.

Secondary Sources

1. Collins, Roger. Caliphs and Kings: Spain, 796-1031. Wiley-Blackwell, 2014.

2. Fletcher, Richard. "Moorish Spain." University of California Press, 2006.

3. O'Callaghan, Joseph F. "A History of Medieval Spain". Cornell University Press, 2013.

4. Reilly, Bernard F. "The Medieval Spains." Cambridge University Press, 1993.

Cultural and Artistic Studies

1. Dodds, Jerrilynn D. "Architecture and Ideology in Early Medieval Spain." Pennsylvania State University Press, 1990.

2. Glick, Thomas F. "Islamic and Christian Spain in the Early Middle Ages." Princeton University Press, 2015.

Further Reading

1. Barton, Simon. "Conquerors, Brides, and Concubines: Interfaith Relations and Social Power in Medieval Iberia." University of Pennsylvania Press, 2015.

2. Catlos, Brian A. "Kingdoms of Faith: A New History of Islamic Spain." Basic Books, 2018.

3. Menocal, María Rosa. "The Ornament of the World: How Muslims, Jews, and Christians Created a Culture of Tolerance in Medieval Spain. Little, Brown and Company, 2002.